Archaeology and the Bible:

Ten Illuminations of Selected Biblical Texts

Patrick Hunt

STONE TOWER PRESS

Stone Tower Press
7 Ellen Rd.
Middletown, RI 02842
stonetowerpress.com

Paperback ISBN: 978-1-7345859-0-2

Formatting and cover design by Amy Cole, JPL Design Solutions

Maps by A. D. Riddle, RiddleMaps.com

The cover image contains a detail of Sennacherib's Prism, British Museum, photo P. Hunt, 2019.

Printed in the United States of America

Second Printing

Table of Contents

❖

Preface

❖

"...Neither was there such a person as Ninus...but that Ninus should have erected on the Tigris at the distance of only forty leagues from Babylon a city named Nineveh, of so great an extent, this has but very little the air of probability...The imaginary empire of Assyria was not yet in existence at the time Jonah is introduced."

Voltaire, *The Philosophy of History*, 1765[1]

Archaeology as an increasingly formal discipline since the 18th century owes much to curious inquiry about the literal, physical places of the Bible, which was widely read and followed at the time publicly and privately as well as in academic circles. Some adventurers such as the Swiss explorer Johann Burckhardt (1784-1817), most famous as the discoverer of lost and forgotten Petra in 1812, traveled for a decade around Palestine, Jordan, and Syria examining biblical sites and was intent on finding more about Edom, Moab, and Ammon. As W. M. Leake in the subsequent Editor's Preface to Burckhardt's 1822 *Travels in Syria and the Holy Land* states posthumously about Burckhardt's discoveries: "He has greatly improved our knowledge of Sacred Geography, by ascertaining many of the Hebrew sites in the once populous but now deserted region, formerly known by the names of Edom, Moab, Ammon and the country of the Amorites."[2]

Despite the above skepticism of Voltaire, other early practitioners include British pioneer archaeologist Austen Henry Layard (1817-1894) intensively searched for Nineveh and proved its location at Kyunjik along with finding there some of the archives of Ashurbanipal's Library.[3] Layard's interest was partly due to Nineveh as a famous toponym from prophetic texts and stories in the books of Jonah, Isaiah and Nahum when the Enlightenment and Voltaire had relegated Nineveh to near mythological status.

To a certain extent, many early archaeology discoveries coincided with a fascination for materially documenting biblical and other ancient texts once it was understood soil and related decomposed organic material covered ancient cities—often covered by broken pottery fragments—and these could be partly revealed underneath by subsurface investigation. Such archaeological research gradually became followed more systematically and scientifically.

Although this is necessarily only the briefest of summaries, Greece, Egypt, and Mesopotamia naturally guaranteed a fair share of the focus in pioneering archaeology with great Classical, Egyptian and Near Eastern collections assembled worldwide since Johann Joachim Winckelmann's (1717-1768) time studying and collecting at the Vatican Museums. The Napoleonic Expeditions to Egypt in 1798, filling much of the Louvre Museum in Paris, coincided with the shrinking Ottoman Empire, facilitating many Mesopotamian and Greek forays such as Layard's and those of Paul-Émile Botta (1802-1870), among others like Jean-François Champollion (1790-1832) translating hieroglyphs via the Rosetta Stone with the help of polymath Thomas Young (1773-1829) and followed by Henry Creswicke Rawlinson (1810-1895) resolving cuneiform inscriptions.[4]

Earlier, Pompeii and Herculaneum, discoveries from the 18th century onward certainly fueled the passion for understanding and collecting remains of Roman urban antiquities in Naples as well as other places.[5] Some of the great museums filled with antiquities collections from these seminal, mainly 19th-century expeditions, include the National Archaeology Museum in Naples assembled from early Bourbon royal collections, the Louvre in Paris, the British Museum in London, Berlin's Pergamon Museum along with its Altes and Neues Museums, and Munich's Glyptotek, as well as the Hermitage in St. Petersburg, the Egyptian Museum in Torino, and the Metropolitan Museum of Art in New York. By the mid- to late 19th century, earlier royal, princely and prelate collectors gave way to private industrialists and other wealthy collectors whose bequests eventually filled these and other museums such as the J. Paul Getty Museum in Los Angeles, itself only founded in 1953.

The German Archaeological Institute (Deutsche Archäologisches Institut) began in 1832 and was followed by the French School at Athens (École française d'Athènes) in 1846. American pioneer scholar Edward Robinson (1794-1863), often termed the founder of "Biblical Geography," initiated Jerusalem explorations around the Temple area and his work there was followed by British officers Charles W. Wilson (1836-1905) and Charles Warren (1840-1927). The Palestine Exploration Fund began in 1865 with Queen Victoria's patronage. The Archaeological Institute of America consortium was founded in 1879 and the American School of Classical Studies at Athens began in 1881, both founded by Harvard University's Charles Eliot Norton (1827-1908), followed by the British School at Athens in 1886; most of these institutions having a focus on Classical Archaeology of Ancient Greece and Rome. The American Academy in Rome was founded in 1894. The American Schools of Oriental Research was founded in 1900. Heinrich Schliemann's startling visionary yet misguided forays at Troy and Mycenae in the last third of the 19th century were followed by more scientific expeditions as archaeology became a formal discipline with input from architects and surveyors. Even Schliemann's 1875 title *Troy and Its Remains* deliberately echoed Layard's Nineveh volume's title with the same publisher, John Murray in London. Pioneering Egyptologist William Matthew Flinders Petrie (1853-1942), originally trained as a surveyor, established a more rigorous approach to archaeology and ceramic studies among other notable contributions in archaeological methodology.

Yet, even into the early 20th century museums, universities, and seminaries concentrated enormous resources toward what became known as "Biblical Archaeology" as a discipline by itself and eventually several publications were published catering to that demand for archaeological knowledge about biblical places. William Foxwell Albright (1891-1971) at Johns Hopkins University helped establish the American Schools of Oriental Research Center in Jerusalem. One of his valued students was George Ernest Wright (1909-1974), an ordained minister who also taught at Harvard Divinity School from 1958 until his death, where he also helped curate the Harvard Semitic Museum from 1961 onward.

Nelson Glueck (1900-1971) was another seminal archaeologist in the Jordan area (however his interpretations have fared since). Yigael Yadin, born Yigael Sukenik (1917-1984), the son of Hebrew scholar Eleazar Sukenik (1889-1953), is one of the most famous names of 20th-century Israeli archaeologists (also military leader). Yadin was vital for the 1954 acquisition by Israel of some of the most important Dead Sea Scrolls—a huge stimulus for archaeology and Biblical studies since 1948; arguably one of the most important biblical discoveries of the 20th century and possibly of all time.[6] He was a principal excavator of Masada, among other sites including Qumran and Hazor. Yadin's pioneering counterpart in Israeli archaeology was Yohanon Aharoni (1919-1976) at Tel Aviv University. Gabriel Barkay (1945-) and David Ussishkian (1935-) are other eminent Israeli archaeologists whose legacies and work continue to be important.

Catering to insatiable appetites for an archaeology especially of the Bible, the American Society for Oriental Research began publishing *Biblical Archaeologist* in 1938, continuing until 1997, when it became the journal *Near Eastern Archaeology.* The Biblical Archaeological Society under visionary Hershel Shanks began publishing *Biblical Archaeology Review* in 1975 as a popular forum focusing on the dialogue between archaeologists and a hungry public.

While Albright's presuppositions as a "maximalist" supporting biblical historicity were never universally held, he is nonetheless acknowledged as the pioneer of "Biblical Archaeology."[7] Today, the term "Biblical Archaeology" à la Albright and his followers is a misnomer for many who may find it a possible oxymoron. Coupling a religious adjective in "Biblical" to a noun in "Archaeology" that aims for scientific precision is understandably problematic. Especially of concern is the precarious historicity of the biblical texts, compounded by narratives that are unquestionably supernatural. This mixing of documented history and the supernatural is too much for many, so they throw out the proverbial "baby with the bathwater," which is no doubt excessive. William Dever (1933-) has been one of the advocates for the clarification of the nomenclature in defining (and also excising) what the word "biblical" as a religious descriptor for what this branch of "archaeology" might entail.

There remain today "maximalists" in the vein of Albright, respected emeritus scholars such as Alan Millard at University of Liverpool, who along with Egyptologist colleague Kenneth Kitchen, maintains biblical historicity. Maximalist predecessors following Albright include Donald J. Wiseman (1918-2010) and Edwin Yamauchi (1937-). There are also, however, in needed counterbalance, equally-respected "minimalist" scholars like Israel Finkelstein of Tel Aviv University, co-director of the Megiddo Excavations since 1994. Although, many would see Finkelstein as more centrist than radical minimalists like Thomas L. Thompson (1939-) and Jon Van Seters (1935-), who in general, rejected any biblical historicity. Unfortunately, such simplistic or marginalizing terms as "maximalist" and "minimalist" are too arbitrary; along the broad spectrum many of us might find some problematic biblical texts needing better translations or interpretations.

If it is possible to get through the gauntlet of Finkelstein's razor-sharp critical logic, biblical scholarship in archaeology survives fairly intact pending ultimate verification. Finkelstein teamed with co-author Neil Asher Silberman in the iconoclastic and groundbreaking *The Bible Unearthed: Archaeology's New Vision of Ancient Israel and the Origin of Sacred Texts* (2001), which has remained a provocative critical "minimalist" text (although now slightly dated and followed by other volumes published by the Free Press and Society for Biblical Literature in 2006 and 2007 respectively). Finkelstein is the primary exponent of the "Low Chronology" that assumes a later Iron Age sequence for the formation of Israel as a national entity from the 10th century BCE onward and, while acknowledging the historicity of David and his family, finds much of the biblical narrative of David and the United Kingdom ideological and after the fact.

Not all agree with Finkelstein and notable critics have included Amnon Ben-Tor and William Dever.[8] Although at times a co-author, Amihai Mazaar often took issue with Finkelstein, believing the truth lay somewhere in the middle between minimalism and maximalism about biblical historicity.[9] Naturally, the pendulum continues to swing back and forth between minimalist and maximalist interpretations as Eilat Mazar in Jerusalem (daughter of Amihai Mazar) and others like Yosef Garfinkel and Saar Ganor at Khirbet Qeiyafa continue archaeological investigations supporting biblical historicity for the Davidic Period. Time will tell if this possible biblical historicity holds up and what will be its reception.

Many archaeological texts of biblical relevance deserve mention but only a few are noted here. Israeli eminent archaeologist Amihai Mazar's *Archaeology of the Land of the Bible* (1990) remains a pillar text of archaeology for several generations with frequent revisions out of his Hebrew University, Jerusalem projects. Eric Cline, certainly among the most prominent American archaeologists along with Jodi Magness and Eric Meyer, has worked decades in Israel at Megiddo and Tel Kabri, among many other projects. His books include both popular and academic tomes. Cline's *Biblical Archaeology: A Very Short Introduction* (2009) is a succinct 168-page treasure. In that work's Epilogue, Cline notes: "Having overcome the sabotaging nihilism of the 1990s and the early part of the new millennium, and notwithstanding the ongoing debates regarding David and Solomon…biblical archaeology continues to benefit from new discoveries, especially ancient writing."[10] Cline then enumerates a few new philological discoveries, including a Philistine inscription from Gath that approximates Goliath's name, the oldest Hebrew abecedary from Tel Zayit, Khirbet Qeiyafa's proto-Hebrew from the 10th century, as well as a few material discoveries including the Jordanian Edomite copper industry at Khirbat en-Nahas that has Solomonic possibilities, and ongoing Jerusalem excavations on the Temple Mount and in the Iron Age Ophel. More than a few others could be enumerated that came after Cline's 2009 publication where the jury is still out on chronology and significance.

On the other hand, Cline's earlier 2007 book, *From Eden to Exile*, justifiably lampoons the credulous behavior of gullible persons who either look to "prove the Bible true"—an impossible task and intellectually suspect as well as having the obvious demerit of lacking faith—in chapters covering biblical mysteries such as Eden, Noah's Ark, the Ark of the Covenant, among other topics. His voice rings clarion:

While doing research for this book, I became amazed and, frankly, appalled by the amount of pseudoscientific nonsense that has been published on these topics…These enthusiasts…all work outside academia. As such, they are not held to the same standards of rigor, peer review, and scrutiny as professional scholars…[11]

Now, about this little book. While I try to be patient often pointing out that Genesis 8:4 doesn't claim "Noah's Ark" landed on Mt. Ararat but on the mountains (plural) associated with what could be read as the region of Ancient Urartu and its Southern Transcausasus empire until collapse in the 7th century BCE[12], I often refer such Ark queries to my dear friend Irving Finkel at the British Museum, who authored *The Ark Before Noah: Decoding the Story of the Flood* (2014). Two other highly recommended books on Biblical Archaeology are by Jonathan Tubb (another British Museum friend) and Rupert Chapman, *Archaeology and the Bible* (1990) and T. C. Mitchell's *The Bible in the British Museum: Interpreting the Evidence* (2004). Tubb and Chapman remind readers how important reading of the Bible was in the early 16th century onward due to its growing availability, which went in tandem with scientific antiquarianism.[13] Although seriously dated, Donald Wiseman and Edwin Yamauchi's *Archaeology and the Bible: An Introductory Study* (1979) is still useful, as have been Yamauchi's caveats about vain attempts to prove the Bible true by a misuse of archaeology.[14]

Influences and possible outright borrowings from other cultures are a given in biblical texts, as attested in the resemblance of more than a few of the Mosaic-Sinaitic Law texts in the *Torah* (especially the *lex talionis* texts) to Hammurabi's Babylonian Law Code of the 19th century BCE, as well as Irving Finkel's studies of Exilic Jews influenced by Mesopotamian narratives such as Gilgamesh and Atrahasis texts, partly surveyed in his book *The Ark before Noah*.[15] In this vein, as previously with my publishing on the borrowing of Phoenician texts in Psalm 48:2-3,[16] we can contemplate the Egyptian long tradition of dream interpretation and the Seven Cows of Heaven roles in chapter/spell 148 of the so-called "Egyptian Book of the Dead" (*Book of the*

Coming Forth by Day) and suggested parallels in Genesis 40-41 in the Joseph narratives as raised here in chapter 2 of this book.

Translations are, of course, the primary textual window to understanding the Bible, with archaeology remaining a secondary window based on materials and their contexts that may illuminate biblical texts. Among common biblical misreadings, it is important to understand the difficulties of translating ancient languages and the four barriers (at least) between us and biblical texts. We are far removed in time, place, language and culture from the biblical authors, so there is likely more than a modicum of problems from "lost in translation" such that some translations need revising almost every other decade due to the volume of research. Mathematicians may be correct in assuming there is no such thing as direct translation since (language) A does not equal (language) B; even linguists might agree. Whether or not some of these textual conundrums are insurmountable obstacles is arguable, but offered here in the following pages are ten selected biblical passages where archaeology can in fact illuminate text. Is it unlikely that archaeology can illuminate every biblical text, but these are just a very few that deserve further attention. If, as happens frequently, these few readings of text and materials together are either premature or wrong, I take full responsibility since archaeology is being updated constantly.

My own background may be relevant. I have published on some biblical texts relative to the Near East (including Phoenician) and lived in Jerusalem as well as Athens during graduate work and beyond. My double undergraduate degree was in Communication Linguistics and Biblical Studies (minoring in physical sciences), my first master's degree was in Biblical Studies, and my Ph.D. in 1991 was in Archaeology (e.g., Archaeological Science), the latter from the Institute of Archaeology, London, now UCL. I was a graduate intern at the U.S. Geological Survey in Menlo Park and a graduate student in 1984 at the American School of Classical Studies, Athens. I did studies at the Institute of Classical Studies, London in papyrology and numismatics in 1988-89, and at the Institute of Archaeology, London in ceramic technology, stone technology and weathering, geoarchaeology (and palynology, metallography of ancient metals, nautical archaeology, and other courses in materials studies between 1986-1988).

I have presented biblical papers at the Organization for the Study of the Old Testament (KUL Leuven 1989, College de France/Sorbonne 1992) and presented related conference lectures at many universities including Katholieke Universiteit Leuven (KUL), Alexander von Humboldt University in Berlin, and at Oxford, U.C. Berkeley, Università ca' Foscari in Venice, among others. A few of my topical biblical publications were by Peeters in Leuven and Peter Lang Verlag in Frankfurt. In 1993 I was listed in *Who's Who in Biblical Studies and Archaeology* by the Biblical Archaeology Society. I was a Post-Doctoral Research Fellow at University of California, Berkeley, in Near Eastern Studies under David Stronach. I continue archaeological research and while teaching since 1993 at Stanford University. I also work for National Geographic, grant sponsor of my research 2007-08, in various capacities including as a National Geographic Expeditions Expert since 2016.

As an archaeologist, I am all too aware of my limitations in biblical languages and the lacunae in my graduate and professional training despite covering a small range of archaeological disciplines including stone technology and deterioration, ceramic technology, and metallography studies. I also hold an appointment as Research Associate at the Institute for EthnoMedicine in Archaeoethnobotany, for which I study ancient plant texts such as Theophrastus, Pliny, and Dioscorides, among others, to be soon published in the *Blackwell Cultural History of Plants* on ancient plant materials and technologies. Thus, the range of topics and materials in this brief book on biblical archaeology and a few selected texts across several millennia therein broadly reflect my professional interests, training, and fascination with the possible role of archaeology to illuminate selected biblical texts.

Patrick Hunt
Stanford University & National Geographic
2019

Endnotes

1   Voltaire, *Philosophy of History*, X, Of the Chaldees, 1765.

2   John Lewis (Johann Ludwig) Burckhardt, *Travels in Syria and the Holy Land*. ed. W. M Leake. London: Association Promoting the Discovery of the Inner Parts of Africa, 1822, v.

3   Austen Henry Layard, *Nineveh and its Remains*. London: John Murray, 1849; Austen Henry Layard, *The Monuments of Nineveh: From Drawings Made on the Spot, First Series*. London: John Murray, 1849; Patrick Hunt, *Ten Discoveries That Rewrote History*. New York: Penguin Group, 2007, ch 3, 45-62.

4   Patrick Hunt, *Ten Discoveries That Rewrote History*. New York: Penguin Group, 2007, ch 1&2, 1-20, 21-44.

5   Hunt, 2007, ch. 6, 109-34; Eric Cline. *Three Stones Make a Wall: The Story of Archaeology*. Princeton: Princeton University Press, 2017, 13ff.

6   Francine Lelièvre, James Snyder, Joel King, eds., *Archaeology from King David to the Dead Sea Scrolls. Collaborative Exhibition in the Montréal Museum of Archaeology and History and the Israel Museum*, Jerusalem, 2003, 21; Hunt, 2007, ch. 7, 135-60, esp. 136, 159-60.

7   Peter D. Feinman, *William Foxwell Albright and the Origins of Biblical Archaeology*. Berrien Springs, MI: Andrews University Press, 2004.

8   Amnon Ben-Tor, "Hazor and the Chronology of Northern Israel: A Reply to Israel Finkelstein." *Bulletin of the American Schools of Oriental Research (BASOR)* 317 (2000) 9-15; William G. Dever, "Excavating the Hebrew Bible or Burying It Again?" (Review of *The Bible Unearthed*). *Bulletin of the American Schools of Oriental Research (BASOR)* 322 (2001) 67-77.

9   Amihai Mazar, "Does Amihai Mazar Agree with Finkelstein's Low Chronology?" *Biblical Archaeology Review* 29.2 (2003); Jennifer Wallace, "Shifting Ground in the Holy Land" *Smithsonian,* May, 2006 where Mazar claims Finkelstein's anti-Solomon dating is "a huge distortion." Also see "Biblical Archaeology," *PBS Religion and Ethics Newsweekly,* Feb. 6, 2004, with interviews of Finkelstein and Mazar, among others (https://www.pbs.org/wnet/religionandethics/2004/02/06/february-6-2004-biblical-archaeology/12501/).

10 Eric Cline, *Biblical Archaeology: A Very Short Introduction,* Oxford, 2009, 131.

11 Eric Cline, *From Eden to Exile: Unraveling Mysteries of the Bible.* Washington, D.C.: National Geographic, 2007, ix.

12 Paul Zimansky, "Xenophon and the Urartian Legacy." *Pallas* 43 (1995) 255-68, esp. 255 where he equates "Ararat" and "Urartu"; Adam T. Smith. "The Making of an Urartian Landscape in Southern Transcaucasia: A Study of Political Architectonics." *American Journal of Archaeology* 103.1 (1999), 45-71.

13 Jonathan Tubb and Rupert Chapman, *Archaeology and there Bible.* London: British Museum Press, 1990, 9ff.

14 Edwin Yamauchi, *The Stones and the Scriptures.* Philadelphia: J. B. Lippincott and Company, 1972, introduction.

15 Irving Finkel, *The Ark before Noah: Decoding the Story of the Flood.* New York: Doubleday, 2014, 226ff.

16 Patrick N. Hunt, "Mt. Saphon in Myth and Fact" in E. Lipinski, ed., *Phoenicia and the Bible. Studia Phoenicia* XI. *Orientalia Lovanensia Analecta* 44, Leuven: Uitgeverij Peeters, 1991, 103-15.

1

An Archaeology of Words: Hebrew Poetry and Word Play in Genesis 1:1-2

❖

Bereishit "In the beginning" opening word in Hebrew Torah scripture or Old Testament Genesis.

An archaeology of words alludes to the original meaning of *archaeologia* from the 18th century before the material discipline of archaeology formally began: it meant a study of ancient words. The richness of word plays in Hebrew illustrates how important ancient words were to those who thoughtfully crafted the scriptures. Although this is not in any way comprehensive, some of my favorite word plays from Hebrew literature show a deliberate use of language for suggesting multiple ambiguities, sometimes even steganographic (hiding things in plain sight), and often paronomasic (having connections in both sound and meaning) ones. Genesis 1:1-2 is one such passage rich in poetic nuances.

Because we have no autograph manuscripts of the oldest biblical texts, we can only guess at the ways in which oral and written texts accumulated together. Sometimes older oral texts are embedded in later texts during the codification process. Before historiography even considered various stages of authorship, acknowledging prior sources would not have mattered, as Herodotus inferred in the beginning of his *History* 1.1, making an effort to distinguish *mythos* (= prehistory) from *historia* when events could be documented. While rather late in biblical history in terms of time lag, the oldest biblical text we have is from a Jerusalem tomb, ca. 600 BCE, and is from Numbers 6. It is the so-called "Priestly Benediction" or "Priestly Blessing" and is discussed at the end of this chapter.

One of the most subtle Hebrew word plays opens up the biblical text. Genesis 1:1 starts out "In the beginning God created...." In the Hebrew word order, the prepositional phrase "in beginning" comes first, followed by the verb "created" where the subject noun "God" comes third. The Hebrew preposition is *be-* (בְּ) for "in" and this is compounded with the word *reishit* (רֵאשִׁית) for "beginning" to create *bereishit* (בְּרֵאשִׁית). The first three Hebrew consonant letters for "in beginning" are *beit* (ב), *reish* (ר), *aleph* (א), exactly the same first three letters of *bārā'* (בָּרָא) for "created" with repeated *beit* (ב), *reish* (ר), *aleph* (א), so when one examines these first two words "In the beginning created" in the Hebrew scriptures, they start out exactly the same. This is highly unlikely to be coincidental and forms a clever paronomasia (sharing sound and meaning[1]) as well as likely being a mnemonic device for the poetic opening of scripture. One of the first to notice this particular opening biblical paronomasia in the Anglophone world was Gary Rendsburg.[2] One could even poetically suggest here that "in beginning" has "created" embedded in it as a form of steganography.

That this phrase is paronomasic with "In the beginning created..." may not be as important as some of its possible purposes such as memorability and the use of poetry to make a theology manifest even nobler by rendering it poetically where the genre of poetry further elevates the register of ideas more than prose for already elevated thought. Other poetic devices embedded in Genesis 1 include the assonance of *tōhû wābōhû* (תֹהוּ וָבֹהוּ) for "formless and empty",[3] along with the repetitions and shared patterns throughout ("And God said", "…Let there be…", "And God saw that it was good", etc.). Another example of assonance in this Genesis 1:1-2 passage, likely also paronomasic given the parallels between sky and water, may be in the euphonic and semantic connection of *shāmayim* (שָׁמַיִם) "heavens" to *māyim* (מַיִם) for "water."

Furthermore, there is a lovely extended poetic figure that functions eidetically (multiple sensory evocation or dramatic intensification as an image[4]) in the imagery of Genesis 1:2b, where "the Spirit of God was hovering over the face of the water." Since the word for "spirit" *rûach* (רוּחַ) can also be used for "breath or wind,"[5] one might be able to visually imagine this by noting, for example, how on a bright day when sunlight shines across a lake, suddenly the wind comes up.

Blowing gently across the sunlit water, the wind breaks up the light into a kaleidoscope of bright fragments with its ripples. One cannot see the wind but one can see what it does, possibly even feel it on the face and hands so that close up it can also be a multi-sensory experience. Like steganography, or hiding things (in this case invisible God?) in otherwise plain sight, the image becomes all the more mysteriously profound because wind itself cannot be seen, only felt, and that instead its effects can be seen in a sensory paradox. Because it also implies movement, this can also be an image of kinesis. Even if this eidetic word picture is not a primary meaning in the passage,[6] it is nonetheless a possible intended ambiguity.

Then, there is the prior image that "darkness was on the face of the deep" in Genesis 1:2a. One more very tentative idea is that the word for "deep" in *tehôm* (תְהוֹם) might refer not only to sea, its customary meaning and primary domain in its other biblical uses. Of course this is not the normal context for this word given the already noted water imagery[7]—although as also mentioned above with *shāmayim: māyim* there is a strong connection between sea and sky—but perhaps it can also suggest here not only looking down but rather also looking up to the huge *abyss* of night sky? Could this be another possible intended multiple ambiguity, often a feature of great poetry?

Summarizing, what if the original material for this prose text was in fact poetry and orally transmitted for some time before written down? It could have been originally all the more memorable—possibly intended to be memorized—as hinted in the few poetic fragments that may remain. What better trope than poetry to express such profound ideas such as "in the beginning" already having "creation" embedded in its first three letters (*b-r-'*) and a sensory subtlety of invisible divine wind hovering across water to gently stir it, especially if light can be seen but not wind, which can only be felt but its effects seen? This is a glimpse into something ineffable.

Oldest Hebrew Inscription

Although unrelated, except as an example of the vagaries of archaeological survival and affirming how difficult it is for both artifact and textual survival from several millennia past, the apparently oldest Hebrew scriptural fragments ever found ca. 600 BCE—thus predating the oldest Dead Sea Scrolls material by at least 400 years—are from Ketef Hinnom, Jerusalem, excavated by Gabriel Barkay in 1979.[8] The Hebrew text was inscribed on rolled up tiny pure silver sheets; one is 10 cm by 2.5 cm (~4 by 1 in.). These must have been part of a necklace and function like *tefillin/phylactories*. The text is called the "Priestly Blessing" or "Priestly Benediction" from Numbers 6: 24-26:

> "The Lord will bless you and keep you. The Lord will make His face to shine upon you and be gracious to you. The Lord will turn His face to you and give you peace."

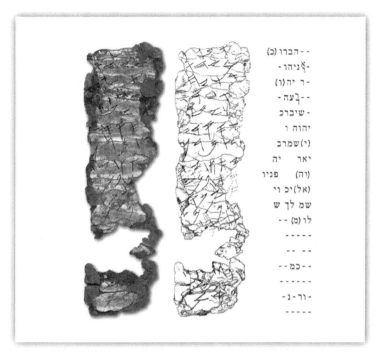

Ketef Hinnom Silver roll, ca. 600 BCE
(Photo courtesy of Gabriel Barkay)

The importance of this archaeological find is underscored by the fidelity of the text with all subsequent texts. It must be remembered that texts are redacted to update language changes, a normal process that most cultures do when dealing with archaized language and subsequent change. Most 21st-century English readers cannot always easily follow Shakespeare, let alone Chaucer, in their original texts; even the King James Bible reflects archaic language needing to be updated, which is why new translations are needed every few generations.

If the original language of the Genesis text might be considerably older than the Iron Age (its cultural background is clearly Bronze Age), which is moot—where possible archaic oral poetic elements exist in the above Genesis 1:1-3 word play-rich passage—then it could also be clear from Genesis that it has been edited about the same date as the Ketef Hinnom textual find: peoples like the Philistines do not yet exist but are mentioned for an updated audience in places such as Genesis 21:32-34: "And Abraham stayed in the land of the Philistines for a long time" (vs. 34).

Of course the date of the biblical text of Genesis, likely an amalgam of different materials, oral and written, is controversial. Yet the Ketef Hinnom silver find of Numbers 6:24-26 easily demonstrates a literate audience ostensibly before the Babylonian Captivity, as do the Arad Letters on clay ostraka—potsherds written by very low-level soldiers,[9] and this Ketef Hinnom silver find evidences a biblical text that is virtually unchanged since, showing long-term textual continuity.

❖

Endnotes Chapter 1

1   Patrick Hunt, "Subtle Paronomasia in the *Canticum Canticorum*: Hidden Treasures of the Superlative Poet" in K.-D. Schunck and M. Augustin, eds. *Goldene Äpfel in silbernen Schalen. Beiträge zur Erforschung des Alten Testaments und des Antiken Judentums* 20. Frankfurt am Main: Peter Lang Verlag, 1992, 147-54.

2   Gary Rendsburg, "Word Play in Biblical Hebrew" in Scott Noegel, ed. *Puns and Pundits: Word Play in the Hebrew Bible and Ancient Near Eastern Literature.* Bethesda, MD: CDL Press, 2000. Rendsburg also notes the unusual syntax/grammar here in Gen. 1:1 and overall poeticism in G. A. Rendsburg, *How The Bible Is Written,* Hendrickson, 2019, 16-26.

3   Also identified as a Hebrew wordplay, cf. Everett Fox et al. *Encyclopedia Judaica* 3, 2007, 2nd ed., 572ff.

4   Patrick Hunt, "Sensory Images in Song of Songs 1:2-2:16," in M. Augustin and K.-D. Schunck, eds. *"Dort ziehen Schiffe dahin..." Beiträge zur Erforschung des Alten Testaments und des Antiken Judentums* 28. Frankfurt am Main: Peter Lang Verlag, 1996, 69-78, esp. 70-1.

5   F. Brown, S. R. Driver, C. A. Briggs, *Hebrew and English Lexicon of the Old Testament.* Oxford: Clarendon Press, (1951) 1994 repr., 924.

6   Note Harry Orlinsky, "The Plain Meaning of RUACH in Gen. 1:2," *Jewish Quarterly Review* 48.2 (1957), 174-82, esp. where he makes the case for interpreting this word as "wind," esp. 177-9.

7   Its earlier Akkadian cognate is *tâmtum* where it is also associated with the chaos of Tiamat. While Tiamat is not so likely intended here, yet neither is it a negation of Tiamat according to D. F. Tsumura, *The Earth and The Waters in Genesis 1 and 2: A Linguistic Investigation.* Sheffield: JSOT Press, 1989.

8   Ketef Hinnom, from Chamber 25, Cave 24. G. Barkay, A.G. Vaughn, M.J. Lundberg and B. Zuckerman, "The Amulets from Ketef Hinnom: A New Edition and Evaluation," *Bulletin of the American Schools of Oriental Research* [*BASOR*] 334 (2004): 41-71.

9   Shira Faigenbaum-Golovin, Arie Shaus, Barak Sober, David Levin, Nadav Na'aman, Benjamin Sass, Eli Turkel, Eli Piasetzky, and Israel Finkelstein, "Algorithmic handwriting analysis of Judah's military correspondence sheds light on composition of biblical texts," *Proceedings of the National Academy of Sciences*, April, 2016; Shmuel Ahituv, "Arad Letters," *Encyclopedia of Hebrew Language and Linguistics*, Leiden: E. J. Brill, 2019 (http://dx.doi.org/10.1163/2212-4241_ehll_EHLL_COM_00000006); "Arad Ostraca, c. 600 BCE" *Center for Online Judaic Studies* (http://cojs.org/arad_ostraca-_c-_600_bce/).

2

Genesis 41,
Joseph in Egypt, and
Pharaoh's Dream of Seven Cows

❖

*Papyrus of Ani, Book of the Dead ch. 148, ca. 1250 BCE, 19th
Dyn., Seven Cows of Heaven, providing bread and beer in afterlife*

"And Pharaoh said unto Joseph, In my dream, behold, I
stood upon the bank of the river: And, behold, there came
up out of the river seven cows, fat fleshed and well favored;
and they fed in a meadow: And, behold, seven other cows
came up after them, poor and very ill favored and emaciated,

such as I never saw in all the land of Egypt for badness: And the lean and the ill favored cows ate up the first seven fat cows: And when they had swallowed, it could not be seen that they had eaten them; but they were still ill favored, as at the beginning. So I awoke. And I saw in my dream, and, behold, seven ears of grain came up in one stalk, full and good: And, behold, seven ears, withered, thin, and blasted with the east wind, sprung up after them: And the thin ears devoured the seven good ears: and I told this unto the magicians; but there was none that could declare it to me."

Genesis 41:17-24

The context of Pharaoh's famous biblical narrative dream is far more Egyptian than it first appears. While seven cows and seven ears of grain are not in themselves necessarily recognized as uniquely Egyptian despite the biblical dream attribution to an unnamed Egyptian ruler, there is nonetheless a long tradition of Egyptian religious motif and imagery more than tenuously connecting this dream narrative in Genesis to Egyptian antecedents in the Egyptian *Book of the Dead* (*Book of Coming Forth by Day*) and Chapter 148 therein where the Seven Celestial Cows of Egypt provision bread and beer—both obvious grain products—in the afterlife. In addition the predictive function of the Seven Hathors also link in prolepsis to this literary dream episode. This chapter outlines the background and the suggested connections that predate the Hebrew text but not necessarily the story behind it.

Following much earlier *Pyramid Texts* and *Coffin Texts* (5th to 8th Dynasty) and *Coffin Texts* (Late 6th Dynasty to 12th Dynasty and beyond) from both Old Kingdom and Middle Kingdom (ca. 2600-1700 BCE),[1] the extant copies of the Egyptian *Book of the Dead* have only survived in the New Kingdom (from 17th Dynasty onward, ca. 1500-1100 BCE) and even into the Ptolemaic Era (ca. 300-100 BCE) to collect as many as possible of the chapters or spells to aid the dead so that they have a safe and productive journey through their ordeals to arrive in the Fields of the Blessed for eternity. But what we have today as the Egyptian *Book of the Dead* is an edited amalgam from the 19th c. of a variety of spells, since no extant papyrus manuscript "book" is identical.[2] The earliest spells like Chapter 30b regarding the so-called "Negative Testimony" (where the deceased confirms not having committed a litany of sins and the sealing the lips are early indeed; the latest chapters up to around 200 are seemingly add-ons accumulating by the reign of the Greek Ptolemies. Chapter 148 of the Seven Celestial Cows seems not to appear codified until the New Kingdom, with the earliest visual examples being the Papyrus of Nakht in the British Museum ca. 1300 BCE, although some of it may appear as early as the time of Djedefohr, half-brother of Khafra-Chephren (4th Dynasty, ca. 2570 BCE) on a quartzite block from Hermopolis.[3]

This vignette also appears in tomb paintings of the 19th Dynasty such as that of Queen Nefertari, wife of Rameses II, in the Valley of the Queens, ca. 1290-24 BCE.

The Cow of the West, patron of Theban Necropolis, Hathor Cow, 19th Dynasty Deer el-Medina Tomb of Amenemipet (wearing solar disc, flail, menat collar)

Chapter 148 specifically is a prayer or incantation spell to ensure the deceased is provided bread (or generic food) and beer, usually from barley, but also wheat grain[4] in the afterlife by the Seven Celestial Cows or Seven Cows of Heaven, whom the deceased must mention by name, since each is specifically named in the Chapter 148 text and often fairly adjacent to their visual image. A table appears in the earlier visual vignettes accompanying the spell but often disappears in the Ptolemaic copies, usually interpreted as an offering table, but the fact that its simplest images contain loaves of bread around a jug of beer duplicates in pictorial form what the heavenly cows provide the deceased iterates the basic provisioning. It is possible that a dedicated beer jug with Egyptian blue pigment was used in a special "bread-and-beer" ritual connected to this chapter based on a New Kingdom find in the Royal Ontario Museum.[5]

Cows and cattle appear frequently in Egyptian art by themselves as symbols of animal husbandry and wealth as well as being symbolic of sacred animals. For example, early images show cattle being herded in the 6th Dynasty limestone relief from the mastaba tomb of Kagemni from Saqqara and also the 18th Dynasty tomb chapel paintings of Nebamun in the British Museum where they are painted on double panels on top of each other. According to the archaeological record, cattle are already attested in the 5th millennium BCE in the Egyptian Fayyum culture.[6] For religious imagery of cattle, "cattle played an important part in the sphere of religion" where the "cow was the incarnation of the great goddesses Hathor, Isis and Nut," the latter symbolizing the sky.[7] The iconic royal aspects of the god Osiris holding crook (*heka*) and flail (*nekhakha* flabellum) folded across his chest also evolved via images of divine kingship where animal herds, especially cattle, are mobilary wealth associated with rulers whose herds must be the greatest as gauges of power, derived from Pre-Dynastic Egypt when animal husbandry and control thereof became a vital Nilotic cultural value.[8] According to Shaw and Nicholson, "The most prominent items in the royal regalia were the so-called 'crook' (*heka*), actually a scepter symbolizing 'government' and the 'flail'…"[9] Since the Pre-Dynastic period of the Neolithic onward, cattle became the most common domesticated herd animal, variously reared for meat, for plowing as draft beasts of burden, for ritual sacrifice and for milk; they were raised in bulk in temple domains as well as on royal and aristocratic estates.[10]

In Ancient Egypt the single hybrid Hathor, the Cow Goddess, is an important deity with her cultic complex at Dendera somewhat associated with a Mother Goddess tradition,[11] as an early cosmic goddess and principal female counterpart of the sun-god Ra as "Mother of the World."[12] Hathor's large place in Egyptian religion is complex and vast, too broad in scale and references to summarize here. One of the earliest known Hathor (or Bat) hybrid cow-woman images is found on both sides of the top of the Narmer Palette from the Early Dynastic period circa 3100 BCE.[13] Hathor is often called the Lady of the West as a funerary deity and yet nurturing goddess whose sculpted images also suckle young pharaohs in New Kingdom pieces, as in the 18th Dynasty Deir el-Bahari chapel of Amenhotep II in the Egyptian Museum of Cairo or the 19th Dynasty Hathor Cow Goddess protecting Ramesses II beneath her dewlap from Deir el-Medina in the Louvre.[14] Hathor's iconography, and that of the *Hesat* Sacred Cow, includes a solar disc between her cow horns and at times in her seated cow form, sometimes on a plinth, wearing a sacred *menat* collar; also the flail over her back and *shuty* "double plumes" over her solar disc can appear, the latter sometimes associated with Maat as Goddess of Justice. Each of these identifying marks often show in the Seven Cows of Heaven vignettes; but the total image is also identified hieroglyphically (flail, solar disc, *menat* collar, *shuty* double plumes) as found in Gardiner's *Hesat* sacred cow hieroglyph.[15]

Tomb of Nefertari, XIX Dynasty, ca. 1290-1224 BCE,
fresco in second chamber, Valley of Queens

Although most likely peripheral, there is another Egyptian tradition of the Seven Hathors that appear at the birth of Egyptians and predict the basic future of that person. Wallis Budge summarizes these Seven Hathors—aggregates of the local Hathors of Thebes, Heliopolis, Aphroditopolis, Sinai, Momemphis, Herakleopolis, and Keset—who were worshipped at Dendera and could be represented as young women with solar discs between cow horns.[16] The Seven Hathors appear in the New Kingdom "Tale of Two Brothers" from *Papyrus D'Orbiney* (British Museum Papyrus EA10183), where they act prophetically in announcing the fates of children, ostensibly at birth, but here, after Khnum creates a new wife for the elder brother to replace his unfaithful wife. Lichtheim also draws the close parallels between this story of the unfaithful wife of the elder brother (Anubis)—who seeks to seduce the younger brother (Bata) and then falsely accuses him—with the Genesis 39 story of Joseph and Potiphar's wife. She notes: "The episode of Bata and his brother's wife has a remarkable similarity with the tale of Joseph and

Potiphar's wife..."[17] (which just precedes the Genesis 41 narrative of Pharaoh's Dream discussed here). The juxtaposition of these two close Egyptian narratives in Genesis does not seem coincidental but helps to promote an Egyptian literary context in the biblical narrative. Here is the "Tale of Two Brothers" passage featuring the Seven Hathors in their predictive function:

> Then Khnum made a companion for him who was more beautiful in body than any woman in the whole land for [the fluid of] every god was in her. Then the Seven Hathors came [to] see her and they said with one voice, "She will die by the knife."[18]

This idea of seven predictive cows, coupled with the provisioning of bread and beer in the afterlife of the Seven Celestial Cows (how close are they to being the same?), parallels somewhat the Dream of Pharaoh in Genesis 41. So what is the tradition of dream interpretation in Egypt and how does this also relate to the Genesis 41 narrative?

Dream books exist in Egypt like in many other ancient cultures, with priestly dream interpreters. "Dreams played an important role in Egyptian culture, principally because they were thought to serve as a means of communicating the will of the gods and serving as clues to future events."[19] One such dream book is the British Museum Papyrus Chester Beatty III, a 19th Dynasty hieratic papyrus recounting many dreams whose interpretations are often based on word play (paronomasic puns), a document from the Ramesside "Deir el-Medina Library."[20]

Although the Papyrus Chester Beatty III is perhaps only one of two dream books to have survived intact, individual dreams and interpretations (*oneiroscopy* in later Greek) are recorded from different periods, e.g., stanzas 9 and 31 in the 12th Dynasty *Tale of Sinuhe,* the Dream of Senuswret I and the Royal Dream Stele of Thutmose IV in front of Giza's Great Sphinx, as well as the military dream of Amenhotep II, among others.[21] The dreams describe what is dreamed and then what the interpretation is with either a "good" or "bad" meaning. This Chester Beatty III dream book is early 13th c. BCE but may reflect compilation as far back as Middle Kingdom (2055-1650 BCE).[22]

Papyrus Chester Beatty—Dream Book Dynasty 19
(Courtesy British Museum)

Here are the selected Chester Beatty III excerpted dream scenarios that have either food, cow or grain imagery, some of whose interpretations are based on homophonic or paronomasic word plays with similar Egyptian phonograms:

"IF A MAN SEE HIMSELF IN A DREAM:
2,14 … seeing the god who is above, GOOD, it means much food…
5,16 … having connexion with a cow, GOOD, passing a happy day in his house…
6,2 … cultivating herbs, GOOD, it means finding victuals…
6,3 … bringing in the cattle, GOOD, the assembling of people for him by his god…
6,7 … threshing grain upon the threshing floor, GOOD, the giving of life to him in his house…
6,18 … seeing barley and spelt [given?] to those yonder, GOOD, it means the protection of him by his god…
8,20 … feeding cattle, BAD, it means roaming the earth…
9,24 … pounding barley or spelt, BAD, the requirement of what he has…"

Note that the biblical Pharaonic dream recorded in the Genesis 41 narrative does not appear in this Chester Beatty III compilation. Thus, although conjectural, if a Pharaoh had experienced a dream like this one recorded in Genesis 41, there may have been no parallel dream to compare when consulting the Egyptian dream books, and such an outcome could have flummoxed the dream-interpreting priests.

Summarizing all the seeming parallels between the Genesis 41 narrative and known Egyptian tradition, the table below suggests strong correlation without implying causation.

	EGYPTIAN Tradition	GENESIS 41 narrative
Nature	cow form, bread & beer (from grain)	cow form heads of grain
Number	7	7
Function	afterlife provision	future provision
Omen	predictive (Seven Hathors)	predictive (as a dream)
Dream Motif	unknown (or not surviving) but oneiroscopy accepted	unknown but Joseph's oneiroscopy accepted

In other words, the comparanda in both accounts have seven cows connected to grain (or its products), both accounts are predictive and about future provisioning, and while the Egyptian tradition does not record this specific pharaonic dream, such narratives of important pharaonic dreams occur and are recorded in some detail in Egypt (cited above in the examples of Amenemhet I and Senuswret I, Amenhotep II, Thutmose IV) where dream interpretation (oneiroscopy) is an acceptable royal custom.

Asking why these parallels (that seem uncoincidental) might occur in both traditions or accounts is not easy to answer. Literary compilers in biblical narratives are anonymous, whereas Egyptian scribal tradition may be attributed or may be anonymous but Egyptian scribes were often highly placed in the social hierarchy where literacy was a vital hierarchical (i.e., royal, religious and aristocratic) privilege for "elites" including those climbing the bureaucratic ladder, since scribal training required considerable means.[23] Elaborate tombs of highly-placed scribes—like the New Kingdom tomb of Khonsu, Dynasty 18 royal scribe of Amenhotep III (ca.1386-53 BCE)[24]—confirm this social hierarchy even when so many Egyptian texts are anonymous. It is logical to assume any oneiroscopic dream interpreting priest-scribes of Egypt would have needed to be literate to consult such dream books for precedents, including such a hypothetical dream like the one in Genesis 41 because the dreamer was a pharaoh in the biblical narrative.

A primary conclusion offered here is that the narrative context of Genesis 41 provides credible Egyptian detail. It is not unreasonable to ask whether this detail supports the Egyptian context of Exodus: the narration so easily fits Egypt and knowledge thereof that the biblical background seems to convey deep knowledge of Egypt, perhaps likeliest from more than casual residence in Egypt. While the correlation-causation question cannot be answered: which version might have influenced the other or which narrative was borrowed, if at all (admittedly a complex problem due to debatable chronology about which account is older). Nonetheless, the multilayered parallels seem to suggest more than coincidental connections between Egyptian tradition and the Genesis 41 narrative. At the very least these connections can be understood if we accept the Genesis attempt at literary historicity, which assumes some familiarity with New Kingdom Egyptian tradition on the part of the Genesis narrative author of a sufficiently Egyptianized vignette.

❖

Endnotes Chapter 2

1   Stephen Quirk and Jeffrey Spencer, eds., *The British Museum Book of Ancient Egypt*. London: Thames and Hudson/British Museum Press, 2001 ed., 97.

2   E.A.T. Wallis Budge, *The Egyptian Book of the Dead*, edited by John Romer. London: Penguin Books, 2008 ed., xxvi.

3   Nicholas Grimal, tr. Ian Shaw, *A History of Ancient Egypt*. Oxford: Blackwell, 1992, 79.

4   R. T. Rundle Clark, *Myth and Symbol in Ancient Egypt*. London Thames and Hudson, 183; Patrick McGovern. *Ancient Brews: Rediscovered and Recreated*. W. W. Norton, 2017, 108.

5   Patrick McGovern,"Barley Beer" Penn Museum. (https://www.penn.museum/sites/biomoleculararchaeology1/resources/ancient-beer/).

6   Douglas Brewer, Donald Redford, Susan Redford, *Domestic Plants and Animals: The Egyptian Origins*. Warminster: Aris and Phillips, 1994, 77-90; "Cattle in Ancient Egypt," Digital Egypt, Institute of Archaeology, UCL (https://www.ucl.ac.uk/museums-static/digitalegypt/foodproduction/cattle.html).

7   Philippe Germond, *An Egyptian Bestiary*. London: Thames and Hudson, 2001, 150, 151-4.

8   Patrick Hunt, "Egyptian Kingship and Animal Husbandry." *Electrum Magazine*, June 2014. (http://www.electrummagazine.com/2014/06/egyptian-kingship-and-animal-husbandry/).

9   Ian Shaw and Paul Nicholson, eds., *The Dictionary of Ancient Egypt*. London: Abrams and British Museum Press, 75.

10 Miriam Stead. *Egyptian Life*, London: British Museum Press, 1994 impr., 33., Shaw and Nicholson, 33.

11 Rundle Clark, 87-9.

12 E. A. Wallis Budge, *The Gods of the Egyptians*, vol. 1. Studies in Egyptian Mythology. Methuen, 1904. Chapter XIV: "Hathor and the Hathor-goddesses," 429, 431.

13 Cyril Aldred, *Egypt to the End of the Old Kingdom*. New York: McGraw-Hill, 1974 repr., 43.

14 Germond, 150.

15 Alan Gardiner, *Egyptian Grammar*. Oxford: Griffith Institute, Ashmolean Museum, 1988, 3rd ed rev., 582.

16 Wallis Budge, *Gods of the Egyptians*, 433-34.

17 Miriam Lichtheim, *Ancient Egyptian Literature*. Vol. II. New Kingdom, Berkeley: University of California Press, 1976, 207.

18 Cited in Lichtheim, 207.

19 Shaw and Nicholson, *Dictionary of Ancient Egypt*, 87.

20 British Museum Papyrus, (EA10683,3); Quirk and Spencer, 2001, 133.

21 J. D. Ray, *The archive of Hor*. (Excavations at North Saqqara) Ostraka texts. London: Egyptian Exploration Society, 1976, 130-6; Quirk and Spencer, 2001, 74, 84; Scott Noegel, "On Puns and Divination: Egyptian Dream Exegesis from a Comparative Perspective" ch. 6, 95-120 and R. B. Parkinson, "Sinuhe's Dreaming(s): The Texts and Meanings of a Simile," ch. 8, 145-74, both in Kasia Szpakowska,, ed. *Through a Glass Darkly: Magic, Dreams and Prophecy in Ancient Egypt*. Classical Press of Wales, 2006.

22 Shaw and Nicholson, *Dictionary of Ancient Egypt*, 87.

23 R. J. Williams, "Scribal Training in Ancient Egypt," *Journal of the American Oriental Society* 92.2 (1972), 214-221; John Baines. "Literacy and Ancient Egyptian Society." *Man: Journal of the Royal Anthropological Institute of Great Britain and Ireland*, 18.3 (1983), 572-99; Quirke and Spencer, 22-3; John Baines. *Visual and Written*

Culture in Ancient Egypt. Oxford: Oxford University Press, 2007, esp. ch. 3, 76-83.

24 Tomb TT-47, el-Khoka necropolis, Thebes; "Royal Scribe's 3,000-Year-Old Tomb Discovered in Luxor," *Archaeology* magazine, Feb., 2017.

3

Joshua 5:2-3 and Flint Knives:
No Anachronism

❖

Predynastic Gerzean Flint Knives from Egypt, ca. 6-5000 yrs BP
(Image in public domain)

"At that time the Lord said to Joshua, 'Make flint knives and circumcise the Israelites a second time.' So Joshua made flint knives, and circumcised the Israelites at Gibeath-Haaraloth." Joshua 5:2-3

One of the most interesting biblical Hebrew passages in the early accounts of Israelite conquest occurs in Joshua 5:2-3. It is fascinating because it narrates a command of God to use a seemingly archaic material: flint or hard stone, explicitly purposed for circumcising the Israelites who have ended 40 years of wilderness wandering. The following verses 4-7 extend the commentary of why mass circumcision is needed: all of the previous male generation who had left Egypt had died and the males born in the generation of wandering had not yet been circumcised.

This passage in Joshua drew my attention in 1992 because I was speaking in Paris at the 1992 International Organization for the Study of the Old Testament (IOSOT) Conference at the College de France-Sorbonne. It was a plenary session where a question and answer period allowed discussion, including interchange on the above passage. Quite a few commentators were debating whether this passage was an anachronism, a Neolithic throwback to vestigial memory. Allowed to comment, I offered that I found its discussion of flint was extremely pragmatic and perhaps surprisingly "modern" due to my own doctoral lithic research. At the Paris conference I shared from Herodotus (5th c. BCE) that the ancient Egyptians still seemed to use stone knives in mummification processes for making abdominal cuts; Herodotus could have either observed or heard a contemporary account: "Then, making a cut near the flank with a sharp knife of Ethiopian stone [λίθῳ Αἰθιοπικῷ], they take out all the intestines..." [1]

Although it is unknown whether Ethiopian stone mentioned by Herodotus was exclusively obsidian, there are many examples of flint knives in Egyptian material history, such as those in the British Museum collection, among others, e.g., the Pitt Rivers Flint Knife, Egyptian Pre-Dynastic Naqada II, ca. 3200 BCE seen below.

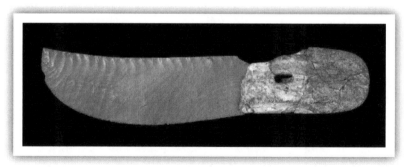

Pitt Rivers Flint Knife, Egyptian Pre-Dynastic Naqada II, ca. 3200 BCE, 24 cm, #EA68512 (Courtesy of the British Museum)

Other flint knives from Egypt are known from the First Dynastic Period (ca. 2960-2770 BCE) in the Pitt Rivers Museum, Oxford, among those illustrated by Flinders Petrie from the Egyptian 12th Dynasty in tools using flint flakes.[2] More important, later Egyptian flint knives from the Late Middle Kingdom to the New Kingdom (likely too many examples to quantify or index) include a 19th Dynasty (ca. 1300 BCE) object from the Ramesseum, Thebes, Egypt, among others annotated by Carolyn Graves-Brown. She argues that "at least until the Early New Kingdom, there is strong evidence that flint weapons were standard military issue, and that far from being a primitive technology, they were a natural choice for both utilitarian and ideological reasons."[3]

This brief following exposition of the Joshua 5 passage and its pragmatism elaborates my 1992 suggestion and commentary from the viewpoint of an archaeologist specializing in stone materials, including a range of silicates from basalt and andesite to flint/chert and other stones.[4]

What arguments can be made for stone tools by examining sharpness and other characteristics? There are considerable reverse engineering studies by archaeologists, among them Payson Sheets, Peter Jones and Dafydd Griffiths, who have experimented with the sharpness of stone cutting tools. Jones affirms that "...simple flakes will provide the sharpest cutting edge in any lithic tool kit."[5] The studies of Payson Sheets with obsidian, including New World cultures like Aztecs, confirm how utilitarian it is relative to metal:

> Obsidian's apparent medical advantage lies in its sharpness. In a detailed study with an electron microscope that magnified the edges of scalpels 50,000 times, only one steel blade approached the keenness of obsidian. Ironically, that blade is no longer marketed because it proved too fragile for normal operating-room use...[6]

Modern medical experimentation for surgical procedures before laser surgery also demonstrate the edge sharpness of stone materials like obsidian and flint that have been around since prehistory: "While they probably never practiced the art of surgery, our Paleolithic ancestors did use tools that have been extolled as more precise than the most modern metal scalpel."[7]

Examining the Joshua 5 passage for "flint knives," the Hebrew uses *harbôt tsurîm* (חַרְבוֹת צֻרִים). Given that the hardest stone available in abundance in the Levant region would be flint, already long purposed in cutting flesh for millennia, this is the logical translation of the material passage. It is also the most logical material to be used in this context given that the narratives, assuming any kind of historicity, do not emphasize a surplus of bronze tools taken by the Israelites migrating out of Egypt, which already had an immensely long flint tool industry for thousands of years, as mentioned above.

In fact, using flint is not only pragmatic as already argued by Graves-Brown, but its mention here suggests this passage is even more historically plausible. Not only would the Israelites not have an abundance of bronze cutting tools for a simultaneous mass circumcision of thousands of males, but bronze cutting edges would not be as sharp as properly knapped flint. Plus, as Stanford University and Institute of Archaeology London students know from first-hand experience, almost any observant group of about 20 moderately trained people can quickly produce hundreds of useable flint microlith blades if sufficient flint core volume can be procured. Microlith flint small blades of a few inches could be reused at least 4-5 times before needing new knapped edges.[8]

In addition, the immediate healing (and possibly the amount of pain produced) of a cut made by flaked flint microliths instead of cast and even sharpened bronze (Ancient Egypt certainly did not possess steel!) also would be much superior to that of any available metal technology of the time. Note that modern studies (below) examining the healing of cuts made with both obsidian and modern surgical steel (flint would not be much less efficacious than obsidian since both stones have acicular and/or lunate fracture with extremely sharp cutting edges); especially apropos here with the sensitive tissue of foreskins. The sharpness of the blade is relevant but most modern users of sheet paper have experienced even paper cuts. One study notes, "Scar width, however, was significantly less in the obsidian wounds [than surgical steel] at 7, 10, and 14 days ($p < 0.005$)...A blinded histologic review suggested that obsidian wounds contained fewer inflammatory cells and less granulation tissue at 7 days."[9]

SEM Images (top) of a single hair cut with obsidian (left) and surgical steel (right);(bottom) the tip of an obsidian blade (left) and a surgical steel blade (right)

Given that this event recorded in the Joshua narrative would hope for quick recuperation, and since bronze blades would create far more tearing of flesh tissue than a sharper stone blade, the narrative appears more pragmatic than otherwise assumed, and more suggestive of a factual underpinning in its detail rather than a mythological literary telling. Note in the above set of SEM images how clean is the cut of a single human hair with obsidian versus surgical steel in the upper micrograph; also note the sharpness of the blade edge of both obsidian and surgical steel in the SEM lower micrograph. Peter Shadbolt states:

At 30 angstroms—a unit of measurement equal to one hundred millionth of a centimeter—an obsidian scalpel can rival diamond in the fineness of its edge. When you consider that most household razor blades are 300-600 angstroms, obsidian can still cut it with the sharpest materials nanotechnology can produce.[10]

Although obsidian should have a smaller cutting edge than flint or chert, flint or chert would still have a exponentially smaller cutting edge than metal technology of the time could produce in bronze blades.

One final added necessary question is how available was flint to the local area in the narrative? The closest toponym mentioned in the expanded text in Joshua 5:9 is Gilgal on the west side of the Jordan Valley, where the event was described as the "Hill of Foreskins" due to the volume of simultaneous mass circumcision where flint microliths could be so easily used. This is extremely germane because Gilgal was occupied as far back as the Neolithic and was situated exactly on a flint ridge:

The [Gilgal] site is located on a low flint ridge and several pediment plateaus of Lisan bed hills 230-240 m below sea level…The Neolithic site, which covers about ten dunams, stretches from the flint ridge to the Lisan plateau…Gilgal:1 Eroded flint ridge which revealed on the summit and along the west slope remains of structures, querns, limestone and basalt tools and flint artifacts.[11]

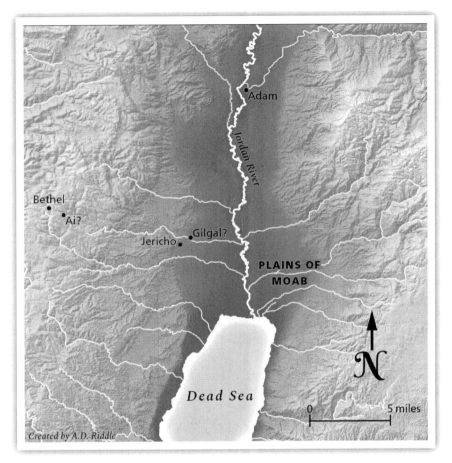

Map of Jordan River Valley with
Neolithic Gilgal site 7 kms from the river

Neolithic Gilgal I has been excavated by Tamar Noy and others with an abundance of flint artifacts noted in the Gilgal publications: "…the flint artifacts were abundant, some of them made of excellent brownish, greyish and purple colored flint."[12] Also note "colored flint…is a common characteristic of the Lower Jordan Valley sites."[13]

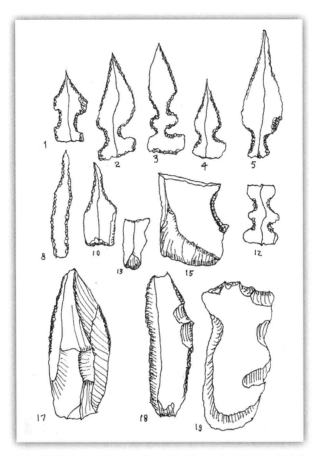

Gilgal I Neolithic Flint artifacts (P. Hunt after T. Noy, 1988)

In conclusion, flint microliths are the most pragmatic tools possible for this Joshua 5 mass circumcision event as narrated, far better than any metal technology at the time, with the best results in abundant procurement for quick use and recuperative and healing time with flint material. This passage also highlights the likely plausibility of this narrative in technological historicity in its logical detail coupled with long-term flint availability near Gilgal as evidenced by archaeological research.

❖

Endnotes Chapter 3

1   Herodotus, *History* 2.86.4. The component of "Ethiopian stone" (λίθῳ Αἰθιοπικῷ) is sometimes referenced as Ethiopian obsidian or other hard silicate stone like flint/chert. Also see Kristina Muller, "Mummies and Surgery: The Story of Ancient Egyptian Obsidian Scalpels." *MedicalExpo* June 9, 2015 (http://emag.medicalexpo. com/article-long/mummies-and-surgery-the-story-of-ancient-egyptian-obsidian-scalpels/). While Robert Kuhn, Egyptologist, Egyptian Museum, Berlin, states in the MedicalExpo article "there is no real evidence that obsidian blades were used in the mummification procedure," on the other hand, there are scores of artifact flint and chert blades from Ancient Egypt, as in the above British Museum flint blade object and in the lead image of Gerzean Neolithic flint blades.

Note the stone knife text again in Gomaa Abdel-Maksouda (Conservation, Cairo University) and Abdel-Rahman El-Amin (Human Remains Lab, Ministry of Egyptian Antiquities) "A Review on the Materials Used During the Mummification Processes in Ancient Egypt," *Mediterranean Archaeology and Archaeometry* 11.2 (2011), 129-150, esp. 131: "...an incision was made on the left side of the abdomen with a knife of obsidian or other kind of stone." Flinders Petrie also records flint flakes embedded in for mining nodules from sandstone as well as flint flakes glued into sickles from the 12th Dynasty (circa 1800 BCE) site of Kahun. See W. M. Flinders Petrie, *Tools and Weapons Illustrated by the Egyptian Collection, University College, London.* British School of Archaeology in Egypt, 1916, 46.

2   B. Asbury, "Rethinking Pitt-Rivers" Pitt Rivers Museum, Oxford University, 2013. (http://web.prm.ox.ac.uk/rpr/index.php/object-biography-index/19-prmcollection/783-flint-knife-188414082/index.html).

3   Carolyn Graves-Brown, "Flint and Forts: the Role of Flint in Late Middle-New Kingdom Egyptian Weaponry," in T. P. Harrison,

E. B. Banning and S. Klassen, eds. *Walls of the Prince: Egyptian Interactions with Southwest Asia in Antiquity*, Culture and History of the Ancient Near East Series, Vol. 77, Leiden: E. J. Brill, 2015, 37ff. Graves-Brown argues that flint weapons were "standard military issue" until the New Kingdom, 37.

4   Patrick Hunt, *Provenance, Weathering and Technology of Selected Archaeological Basalts and Andesites.* Ph.D. Dissertation, Institute of Archaeology, UCL (U. London), 1991. This dissertation followed two graduate internships at U.S. Geological Survey, Menlo Park, 1987-1988 in geological studies.

5   Peter Jones, "Experimental Butchery with Modern Stone Tools and Its Relevance for Palaeolithic Archaeology," *World Archaeology* 12.2 (1988), 153-65.

6   "Doctor, Archeologist Find New Use for Ancient Tool," *Washington Post,* January 1, 1981. The archaeologist in discussion is Payson Sheets, University of Colorado.

7   "Surgeons Use Stone-Age Technology for Delicate Surgery," *University Record,* University of Michigan, September 10, 1997.

8   Professor John Rick at Stanford (now emeritus) regularly conducted flint-knapping sessions for students and colleagues; Dr. Dafydd Griffiths at the Institute of Archaeology, London, also held flint-knapping sessions as has Tomos Proffitt. Currently at UCL, Karl Lee has been conducting flint-knapping master classes, June, 2019 and public events are also available (https://www.instituteofmaking. org.uk/events/detail/member-masterclass-flint-knapping).

9   J. J. Disa, J. Vossoughi, N. H. Goldberg, "A comparison of obsidian and surgical steel scalpel wound healing in rats." *Plastic and Reconstructive Surgery* 92.5 (1993), 884-87.

10   Peter Shadbolt, "How Stone Age blades are still cutting it in modern surgery." *CNN* Online (https://edition.cnn.com/2015/04/02/ health/surgery-scalpels-obsidian/index.html).

11 Tamar Noy, Joseph Schuldenrein and Eitan Tchernov, "Gilgal, A Pre-Pottery Neolithic Site in the Lower Jordan Valley," *Israel Exploration Journal* 30.1/2 (1980), 63-82, esp. 63.

12 Tamar Noy, "Gilgal I—A Pre-Pottery Neolithic Site, Israel,—the 1985-97 Seasons," *Paléorient* 15.1 (1989) Colloque Préhistoire Levant II, 1988, Editions de CNRS, Paris, 1989, 11-18, esp. 12.

13 Footnote 12 on the same page (note 11 above, Noy, 1989).

4

Why Solomon's Legendary Gold is Gone: I Kings 10

❖

Ancient Gold Jewelry, ca. 14th c. BCE *Israel Museum, Jerusalem*

"The weight of the gold that Solomon received in that year was 666 talents, not including the revenues from merchants and traders and from all the Arabian kings and the governors of the territories. King Solomon made two hundred large shields of hammered gold; six hundred shekels of gold went into each shield. He also made three hundred small shields of hammered gold, with three minas of gold in each shield… All King Solomon's goblets were gold, and all the household articles in the Palace of the Forest of Lebanon were pure gold. Nothing was made of silver, because silver was considered of little value in Solomon's days."

I Kings 10:14-17, 21

A question often heard with regard to biblical historicity is that if Solomon's legendary wealth was so great, why has none of it been found by archaeology? The above narrative from I Kings 10 is full of superlative details but is it merely literary hyperbole? Perhaps the first question is more naive about material history and the second one is more sophisticated, but both deserve some attention. This has been addressed elsewhere by good scholarship over previous decades,[1] but fresh archaeological detail has accrued since prior publications about this question, now discussed in this chapter. Scholars like Finkelstein who are skeptical about biblical historicity have every right to argue against the literary account of Solomon as hyperbole, nonetheless the account of Solomon is no more hyperbolic than the records other Ancient Near Eastern rulers claim, as other scholars like Millard who find the Solomon story credible also argue. Is the reality to be found somewhere in the middle or is one side resting on stronger evidence? What are the archaeological circumstances underpinning either side of the debate?

For background context, it is important to remember that archaeology can only reconstruct from the fragments of what remains of the past. Estimates differ widely, but if we now have far less than 5% of even the total material from the Medieval world 1000 years ago, how much less exponentially remains from the Roman world 2000 years ago, likely less than 1% ? Consider that ~25 meters of deposits cover the city of Rome from the Late Republic to the present and that the imperial city of Rome itself measured at least around 3-5 kilometers across from side to side in any direction.[2] If we know that literally thousands of Roman buildings, often with multiple levels, and monuments covered the great city of Rome with a population of around 1 million people around the time of Nero[3] (many of them built in stone after the Great Fire of Rome in 64 CE[4]), how many visibly survive today? Maybe 25 buildings and monuments are sufficiently preserved to easily understand and measure them with the eye. This can include the Pantheon, itself modified, as well as the Colosseum, the Column of Trajan, and the Arch of Constantine, among other monuments. But that total of surviving Roman structures does not include the vast amount of organic objects of wood, textile and other materials now reduced by decomposition to soil. Even if we comprehend how much of Roman life can be documented from the Vesuvius eruption of 79 CE that covered and sealed Pompeii and Herculaneum, this event presents an anomaly of material preservation.[5] Thus, extrapolating the likely exponential loss to reduce the percentage of archaeological remains considerably even greater with another millennium, we have to wonder how little material survives then from the transition of Bronze Age to Iron Age around 3,000 years ago at the putative time of Solomon?

Although Jerusalem was a small city on the Ophel (eastern) Hill under David—possibly only 500 *dunams* or roughly 5,000 people—it was politically expedient to place the capital within the smallest tribe of Benjamin in a neutral buffer zone between the more populous Ephraim and Judah—a "compromise capital."[6] It may not have grown much more under Solomon, but its regional importance did. Several factors suggest that if Solomon indeed ruled Israel a little later than 1000 BCE (possibly 970-931 BCE),[7] there was a power vacuum in the normal Mesopotamian or Egyptian dominance of the Levant, partly due to environmental collapse.[8] It was systemic, however, and not due to any sole causality as invasion, migration, stagnant trade, and warfare also contributed, as "no single cause can explain what happened in all regions and states".[9] Typically when either Egypt or Mesopotamia was powerful, also leaving its cultural footprint on the region, the other was weak.[10] But at the end of the Bronze Age and beginning of the Iron Age around the mid-12th c., both Mesopotamia and Egypt (after Ramesses VI) had essentially collapsed in terms of hegemony over the Levant. As Cline relates:

...[T]he Hittites, the Mycenaeans, the Canaanites, the
Cypriots and others—fell one by one...Egypt became a sec-
ond-rate empire, a mere shadow of what it had once been...
Beyond Egypt, almost all of the other countries and powers
of the second millennium BC in the Aegean and the Near
East - those that had been present in the golden years of
what we now call the Late Bronze Age—withered and disappeared, either immediately or within less than a century.[11]

Likewise in Syria[12] and Mesopotamia, Babylon fell under control
of the Elamites to the southeast, and Assyria retreated to its natural
boundaries after Ashur-bel-kala died (mid-11th c. BCE) with ultimate
Aramean expansion and loss of much Assyrian territory as well as the
Kassite collapse in 1155 BCE.[13] Thus, no sovereign Mesopotamian states
were able to exert power over the Levant after such rulers as Tushratta
of the Mitanni and Assur-uballit of Assyria "made their exits."[14] In that
Ancient Near Eastern power vacuum, Levant states like Israel finally
could assert their independence both politically and economically.

Thus, also in keeping with that period of independence Israel could
have had a virtual monopoly on significant wealth-producing North-
South-East-West trade routes in the Southern Levant. There were two
main north-south connecting routes both along the coast (International
Coastal Highway, also known as the Way of Hor[us] or later Via Maris)
and inland along the Jordan River Valley (Transjordanian Highway)
or on the eastern plateau above it, the latter also called the "King's
Highway" (*Derek Hammelech* in Hebrew*)* mentioned in Numbers
20:17.[15] Furthermore, Jerusalem was another southern nexus link on
both the east-west axis connecting these two north-south routes in the
early Iron Age from the area of Gaza to Jerusalem to the Transjordan
as well as a junction on the central north-south hill route from central
Israel to Bethlehem, Hebron and the Negev; another northern link
was through the Esdraelon Valley via Beth Shean.[16] Some of the documented luxury goods traded included perfumes and spices from the
Red Sea region to the south. This would not only entail trade goods
such as frankincense (*libanon* in Old Hebrew) from the Southern

Arabian peninsula near modern Oman and the offshore island of Socotra, but also balsam (*bosem* in Old Hebrew) as well as myrrh (*mor* in Old Hebrew)[17] along with other spices from further East and south in the Orient, either along the Indian Ocean or Red Sea- East African coasts. These additional spices include cumin and cinnamon, aloes, calamus, henna, spikenard, possibly from the Himalaya, and even saffron. Some have doubted that cumin, for example, was known and traded this early but Mycenaean Linear B Tablets from at least 13th c. BCE have recorded it as *ku-mi-no*.[18] Likewise, the Old Hebrew word for cinnamon is exactly *kinnamon* as seen in the *Shir-Hashirim* (Song of Songs 4:13-16) along with other perfumes and spices.[19] Red Sea trade with India aided by Phoenicia included sandalwood and precious stones such as lapis lazuli, sardonyx and other gems aided by widespread trans-oceanic Phoenician seafaring expertise. Although arguable, some believe the Cochin Jews settled in India at this time and that even silk was also possibly traded by Jews in antiquity.[20]

Perhaps more relevant is the mutually beneficial economic exchange between Hiram of Tyre and Solomon and other commodities. Tyre produced timber and Israel produced agricultural surplus, including olive oil and grain, in a mixed ecomony and both profited thereby.[21] But Solomon also likely had a significant share in the rich copper trade of the Arabah, especially the Timna Valley. New archaeological research in regional mining there shows exactly this economic feature with control possibly ultimately vested in the more powerful state of Israel. Despite the controversial argumentative seesaw that went back and forth for decades beginning with Nelson Glueck and followed by James Muhly, Israel Finkelstein and Beno Rothenberg, new evidence from Thomas Levy's excavations does posit Solomonic Era 10th-9th century BCE chronology—verified by high precision radiocarbon dating—for the rich Jordanian copper mines of Khirbat en-Nahas mines (*nahas* means "copper" in the cognate Semitic languages) of the Faynan district with massive industrial copper slag, an area that was under Edomite control but Solomon seems to have annexed.[22] As Levy notes, "...This research represents a confluence between the archaeological and scientific data and the Bible."[23]

In addition, archaeological research on the Gheralta Plateau in Northern Ethiopia by Louise Schofield, formerly of the British Museum, may have rediscovered the Sabean capital of the legendary Queen of Sheba, literarily partnered with Solomon in I Kings 10:1-10, although as yet unverified despite a rich gold mining find datable from the early first millennium BCE through the 9th-8th c. BCE.[24] Even the biblical reference of Ophir as a land of gold has been corroborated outside biblical texts: in the archaeological finds of the Tel Qasile excavations by Amihai Mazar of the Philistine city in the 1980's—a region that became annexed to Israel under Solomon—is a potsherd from the 11th-10th c. BCE with a famous inscription reading "Ophir gold to Beth Horon, 30 shekels," although some interpret it to mean only that the statement of "Ophir gold" is merely nomenclature distinguishing "fine gold."[25] Nonetheless, the name of Ophir means something valuable as an identified toponym outside biblical literature and reinforces the text.

What about the volume of gold said to accrue to Solomon in I Kings 10:14 in the opening of this chapter? Some earlier translations read "The weight of the gold that Solomon received yearly was 666 talents" but likely the better translation for *beshanah ehat* is likely "in [that] one year," the year of the Queen of Sheba's purported visit with lavish gifts from the enormous gold reserves of Ophir if any such state visit happened, undocumented elsewhere before this passage. The value of a talent fluctuates through history and there is much debate about how to calculate such a value compounded for a volume of 666 talents. A conservative estimate—if the comparable Babylonian talent of the Middle to Late Bronze Age of at least 29 kgs/64 lbs is at all applicable[26]—might mean that Solomon in one particular year (perhaps his best?), could have acquired 42,624 lbs. of gold. In a modern comparison this could be valued (not using Troy ounce weight of 12 ounces per pound but 16 ounces) at roughly $19,000 per pound (assuming $1300 per ounce market value), then multiplying 666 talents x 64 lbs = 42,624 lbs x $19,000 per pound = $809,856,000 million. Of course this is highly subject to fluctuating talent weight. But somewhere near a billion dollars of gold is not at all that enormous a volume in the ancient world. While admittedly a millennium later in the 1st c. BCE with different weights to a talent, Ptolemy XII Auletes of Egypt was to pay Julius Caesar the sum of 6,000 talents of gold to grant it the status of a "Friend and Ally of the Roman People,"[27] an amount around ten times (around $8 billion) to what Solomon is recorded as receiving in that specific year. Although some doubt this Egyptian amount was ever paid out, Westall quotes it as verified in criticism of Caesar by Suetonius (*Iul. Caes.* 54.1-3) for only a portion of his avarice.[28]

Perhaps more apropos is the annual revenue of the Persian emperor Darius I (ca. 550-487 BCE). According to Herodotus in his *History* III. 89-97, if accurate, who tallies the yearly contributions of the individual satrapies in talents, not only did the Indians pay 360 talents of gold dust (*History* III.94.2), but in total Darius annually received 14,560 talents of gold measured in Euböic talents (1 Euböic talent=35.8 kgs/79 lbs) across the Persian Empire, but not counting his Mediterranean vassals.[29] Admittedly, the Persian Empire dwarfs the kingdom of Solomon. Herodotus first makes the conversion from silver to gold (*History* III.95), so if this account of Herodotus is not hyperbolic—apparently far less so than Solomon—Darius annually received $21,854,560,000 billion (14,560 x 79 lbs = 1,150,240 x $19,000) in gold in modern terms, in other words, about 25 times what Solomon is recorded as receiving in that one year.

In any case, this Solomonic wealth—even if only a fraction of the riches of Darius—as recorded in I Kings 10 does not seem out of place with antiquity in comparison. Kitchen agrees with Millard that this description of Solomon's gold in I Kings 10 "was consistent in use and extent with what we know about the ancient Near East."[30] For comparison, Millard cites Tutankhamun's tomb treasure, among other ancient wealth such as the accounts of Alexander in 330 BCE—capturing 1,180 tons of gold at Susa among 40,000 talents of precious metals in total, a seemingly incredible volume that isn't necessarily plausible[31] — along with Assyrian campaigns of Sargon II (765-05 BCE) and his capture of the city of Musasir in Urartu with loot including 25,000 bronze shields and six shields of gold that weighed about 700 lbs or 5 talents. Sargon II's campaign was also depicted similarly in the reliefs at his palace of Dur-Sharrukin (modern Khorsabad).[32] Additionally, Millard cites Thuthmose III's documented gifts to the Karnak Amun Temple as 152,107 *debens* of gold (1 *deben* = 91 gms, 2 *deben* is an Egyptian weight = 182 gms), equal to 13.5 tons, from Thutmose's catalogue on the Amun temple wall covering five rows of description about gold gifts.

Likewise, Assyrian Esharhaddon, son of Sennacherib conquering Nubia records of his conquest of Sidon of Phoenicia that he captured enormous riches including piled-up possessions of gold, silver, precious stones, elephant hides, ivory, ebony, boxwood, colorful garments, linen, all the personal valuables of the King of Sidon, countless people as slaves and huge numbers of herd animals. Esharhaddon's parallel account of conquering the Egyptian the capital of Memphis from Tirhakah, King of Egypt is likewise full of loot, including immense gold, silver, ivory, precious stones, and other treasures gold and silver.[33]

Also, for wealth beyond even accounting, Shalmaneser III on his Black Obelisk, ca. 858-824 BCE, face B, lines 99-102, British Museum, (with the famous "Jehu, some Omri" tribute line face B, 101) claimed "I marched as far as the mountains of Hauran, destroying, tearing down and burning innumerable towns, carrying booty away from them which was beyond counting..."[34] There are so many examples of acquired wealth by conquest from the Ancient Near East of the 1st millennium BCE, especially the Assyrians from their zenith between 9th-7th centuries BCE, that it nearly normalizes the wealth of Solomon, regardless whether more than a few claims might be considered hyperbole. This virtual litany of wealth claims and conquest acquisitions will be examined again with regard to what likely happened to Solomon's gold, of which traces logic suggests archaeology would be unlikely to find much remaining in situ.

So in explaining Solomon's gold wealth as consistent with Ancient Near Eastern tradition, the question remains as to what could have happened to it. Modern Egypt and Persia both have high quantities of gold in their finds from antiquity, Israel does not. But applying the practices of conquests by both Egypt and Mesopotamia, it seems likely any gold holdings acquired by Israel when both Egypt and Mesopotamia were weak would dissipate when either culture became strong again. The first such flexing of Egyptian power came under Shishak in the last third of the 10th c. BCE, specifically; the first such flexing of Mesopotamian muscle returned a few centuries later under the Assyrians in the 9th c. BCE. Both cultures in turn devastated the Levant, and from the accounts already examined it seems logical that they would have stripped Israel of any such precious metals wealth if at all possible as the spoils of war.

Thus, it is no surprise that these accounts of such spoils of war and Israelite or Judean loss are exactly what is claimed in I Kings 14 (and I Chronicles 12) with the Egyptian campaign of Shishak in 926-925 BCE as well as in II Kings 18 (and II Chronicles 28) between 722-704 BCE with the campaigns of Sargon II and Sennacherib and seemingly confirmed or at least implied in the extra-biblical accounts by the Egyptians and the Assyrians themselves, as will be shown shortly.

First, the biblical Shishak account in both I Kings 14 and II Chronicles 12 is seemingly an honest portrayal of the humiliation of the Judean king Rehoboam, son of Solomon, by Shishak of Egypt but lacks corroboration outside the biblical rendering. That Shishak or Sheshonq invaded the Levant is a given.[35] Kitchen, however, reads the biblical texts explicitly as the simplest account of what happened to Solomon's gold,[36] an Occam's Razor explanation, especially as the claim is that Shishak had comprehensive acquisitions from both the temple and royal treasures:

> In the fifth year of King Rehoboam, Shishak king of Egypt attacked Jerusalem. He carried off the treasures of the temple of the Lord and the treasures of the royal palace. He took everything, including all the gold shields Solomon had made. I Kings 14:25-26

The key phrases here in the first biblical account are "carried off treasures" and "took everything." This is an unblunted, caustic record documenting how severe the loss was without any apparent euphemism. The parallel record in II Chronicles offers that and more about why the loss was credible.

> …Shishak king of Egypt attacked Jerusalem in the fifth year of King Rehoboam. With twelve hundred chariots and sixty thousand horsemen and the innumerable troops

of Libyans, Sukkites and Cushites that came with him from Egypt, he captured the fortified cities of Judah and came as far as Jerusalem... When Shishak king of Egypt attacked Jerusalem, he carried off the treasures of the temple of the Lord and the treasures of the royal palace. He took everything, including the gold shields Solomon had made. II Chronicles 12:2b-4, 9

Although II Chronicles 12 duplicates word for word some of I Kings 14:9, it also adds salient details up front regarding the size and makeup of the Egyptian and allied forces. Again, the point to be made is that both biblical accounts emphasize the totality of the gold and related treasures taken away. While there is an Egyptian record, the Bubastite Portal on the Amun Temple at Karnak, of the invasion of the Levant and subsequent humiliation under Sheshonq (the Egyptian rendering of the same name as the biblical Shishak), it is missing quite a few place names across multiple columns and rows that could identify it as the same event that emptied out Jerusalem.

Out of the original 156 place names that were listed, many are destroyed by being chopped out or eroded.[37] A total of only 52 or around a third of the 156 place names are reliably identified with at least 22 place names destroyed and at least 30 incomplete or illegible with at least 34 unidentified. Plus these names are in Egyptian and may bear little resemblance to the place names in other Semitic languages, including the cognate languages of Phoenician and early Hebrew. So it is an argument from silence either way and extremely problematic to conclude that Jerusalem and Judah either are or are not included on the incomplete Bubastite Portal recording Shishak's invasion.

The Bubastite Portal does establish, however, that Shishak was in the region to the immediate north and south of Judah and reasonably close to Jerusalem. But to cite Shishak's Bubastite Portal as evidence from Egypt for or against his taking Jerusalem is not feasible for several reasons in addition to its incompleteness. It has no narrative and is also possibly hyperbolic as well as being "vague and generalized" as Pritchard maintains, adding "It is disappointing to find that the Egyptian texts do not enlarge our understanding of his campaign in Palestine in a sense which constitutes a real addition to the biblical account."[38]

Perhaps the most detailed recording of a historical event relative to Shishak and Jerusalem belong to the biblical accounts of I Kings 14 and II Chronicles 12, although some scholars like Sagrillo and Finkelstein[39] find the whole account lacking historicity for multiple reasons: 1) Egypt could not field such an army and the chariot ranks are exaggerated by a "factor of ten" where the Negev alone (mentioned in the conquest) would be immensely difficult to negotiate for chariots, both if which seem fair enough criticisms. 2) Again the lack of mention of any places in the United Monarchy on the Bubastite Portal is problematic (although a negative argument from silence is not really compelling. 3) According to Finkelstein, the material culture of Judah wasn't sufficiently developed—although this too is more debated and increasingly less a skeptical problem with archaeological research and excavations in Jerusalem and Judah since 2000 that has greatly evidenced more sophistication than previously allowed, including on the Ophel Hill with the City of David and the Judean fortress of Khribet Qeiyafa.[40] Even the best argument from Sagrillo that a more accurate count of Egyptian forces, lowering them significantly, needn't logically contradict the biblical account of Shishak invading the Levant and possibly being the first to ransack Solomonic treasure. Plus, a fragmentary Shishak stela found at Megiddo bearing his cartouche lends credence to Shishak being in the region of Israel.[41]

But this is not the only time Jerusalem might be the focus of an invasion that could have pilfered its wealth. The subsequent Assyrian Empire also invaded under Tiglath-Pileser III (ruled 745-27 BCE) and Sennacherib (740-681 BCE) who, while the latter does not claim actually taking Jerusalem, rather only "shutting up Hezekiah like a bird in a cage," both the biblical accounts and Assyrian records document Jerusalem's loss of wealth in several episodes, including during the reign of Hezekiah's father King Ahaz:

> Tiglath-Pileser king of Assyria came to Ahaz, but he gave
> Ahaz trouble instead of help. Ahaz took some valuable

things from the Temple of the Lord, from the palace, and from the princes, and he gave them to the king of Assyria, but it did not help. II Chronicles 28:20-21

Here in II Chronicles the losses of Ahaz and Jerusalem are not specified other than temple and palace treasure along with some princely loss. But II Kings is much more specific to Hezekiah's loss:

In the fourteenth year of King Hezekiah's reign, Sennacherib king of Assyria attacked all the fortified cities of Judah and captured them. So Hezekiah king of Judah sent this message to the king of Assyria at Lachish: "I have done wrong. Withdraw from me, and I will pay whatever you demand of me." The king of Assyria exacted from Hezekiah king of Judah three hundred talents of silver and thirty talents of gold. So Hezekiah gave him all the silver that was found in the temple of the Lord and in the treasuries of the royal palace. At this time Hezekiah king of Judah stripped off the gold with which he had covered the doors and doorposts of the temple of the Lord, and gave it to the king of Assyria. II Kings 18: 13-16

The latter account of Hezekiah's tribute gives a total of 30 gold talents and 300 silver talents—and historically the two precious metals volumes are often almost equal in value at a 10:1 ratio of silver to gold—but also specifies the sources as all the silver from the temple and the royal palace treasuries and even pinpoints the gold stripped from temple doors and doorposts, presumably not added loss but the same loss in further detail. Again using an Euböic talent weight equivalency if applicable, this translates to 79 lbs. per talent x 30 talents x $19,000 per pound = around $45 million for the gold in modern terms and a likely equal amount of $45 million for the silver given by Hezekiah to Sennacherib as a total of around $90 million in modern terms (of course these valuations are only estimates)—a far cry from Solomonic wealth at around 12% of that total—but if the Egyptian Shishak had already taken the bulk of Jerusalem's wealth, this might make some sense in what had accumulated to Judah in the interim of two centuries. It would not make sense for Sennacherib to take around the same amount Solomon had purportedly acquired, because it would then render the double biblical Shishak accounts in I Kings 14 and II Chronicles 12 as hyperbole or negate that humiliating narrative.

But even more compelling in terms of corroboration is the fact that Sennacherib himself claimed similar amounts taken from Hezekiah in several different Assyrians records, e.g., the Taylor Prism and the Rassam Prism, both in the British Museum. In the Taylor Prism, Sennacherib claims:

> "In addition to 30 talents of gold and 800 talents of silver, [there were] gems, antimony, jewels, large sandu-stones (carnelian?), couches of ivory, house chairs of ivory, elephant's hide, ivory (lit. elephant's "teeth"), maple, boxwood, all kinds of valuable (heavy) treasures..."[42]

The Rassam Prism repeats these details with added quantities listed by Sennacherib:

> [In addition to the] 30 talents of gold, 800 talents of silver, [there were] gems, antimony, jewels, large sandu-stones (carnelian?), couches of ivory, house chairs of ivory, elephant's hide, ivory (lit. elephant's "teeth"), maple, boxwood, colored woolen garments, garments of linen, violet and purple wool, vessels of copper, iron, bronze and lead...[43]

The discrepancy between the biblical account of 1000 talents of silver and Sennacherib's account of 800 talents of silver may be resolvable by adding the value of the other appropriated goods, but this is moot. That the gold volume is identical in all accounts and the silver volume is similar (plus value of other goods) lends credibility and corroboration to both biblical and Assyrian accounts and the overall wealth (no small amount) that the Assyrians acquired from Jerusalem.

Nebuchadnezzar also claimed ample wealth and tribute captured from Jerusalem by Babylon between 604-586 BCE in the *Jerusalem Chronicle ABC 5*,[44] "received its heavy tribute" (Reverse side B, line 13) and also narrated in II Kings 24: 13 in more detail: "As the LORD had declared, Nebuchadnezzar removed all the treasures from the temple of the LORD and from the royal palace, and took away all the gold articles that Solomon king of Israel had made for the temple of the LORD."

Whatever remnant Solomonic gold volume that could possibly be left to the Babylonians is arguable at best, although captured sacred temple objects (gold e.g., goblets) profaned by Belshazzar at his demise do play a role in the supernatural literary narrative of Daniel 5:3ff. and the famous handwriting on the wall vignette. Nonetheless one has to wonder how much Nebuchadnezzar could have found in a seemingly depleted Jerusalem already ransacked by at least two prior invasions.

Yet despite these documented conquests (Egyptian, Assyrian, Babylonian) specified here, they weren't the only invasions of Jerusalem in the 1st millennium BCE. It makes much sense that the following Persian occupation as part of a satrapy, then that of Alexander the Great in the 4th century BCE (333 BCE) and his Seleucid successors into the 2nd century BCE, and also the Romans under Pompey in the mid-1st c. BCE (50 BCE) and any other Romans also would have squeezed every bit of gold out of Jerusalem whenever and wherever possible. Finally, the destruction of Jerusalem by the Romans under Titus in 70 CE would have also added to the spoils extracted from the Jews. So in conclusion, other than a few small hoards buried in times of chaos (whose owners never returned), it would be extremely unlikely anything of Solomon's reputed wealth lasted given the record of invasions and conquest Jerusalem endured over a millennium, as the accompanying map shows. Perhaps this is the best explanation to be expected: however much he might have acquired, regardless of any possible hyperbole in the biblical narratives—even though fairly consistent with Ancient Near Eastern cultures, Solomon's gold is long gone.

❖

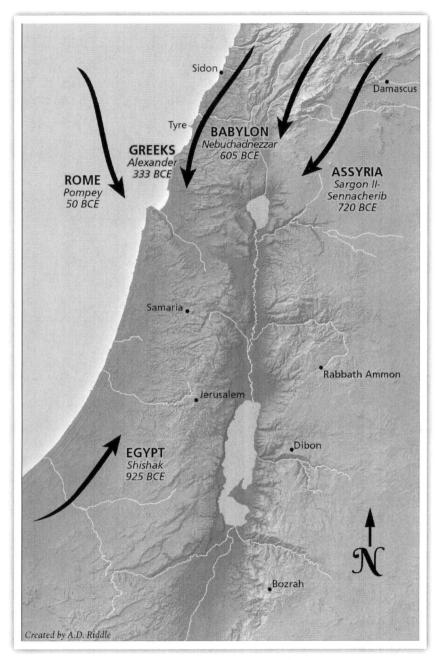

Map of Invasions of Judah/Judea and Jerusalem

Endnotes Chapter 4

1   Alan R. Millard, "Does the Bible Exaggerate King Solomon's Golden Wealth?" *Biblical Archaeology Review* 15.3 (1989), 20-29; Kenneth Kitchen, "Where Did King Solomon's Gold Go?" *Biblical Archaeology Review* 15.3 (1989), 30.

2   Amanda Claridge, *Rome: Oxford Archaeological Guide.* Oxford: Oxford University Press, 1998, 1-2; Filippo Coarelli, *Rome and Environs: An Archaeological Guide.* Berkeley: University of California Press, 2007, 2-9.

3   Alex Scobie, "Rich and Poor in the Roman World, 50 BC–AD 150" *Classical Outlook* 60.2 (1982) 44-46, esp. 44 where Scobie quotes estimates from a minimum of 600,000 to around 1.2 million; Elio Lo Cascio, "The Size of the Roman Population: Beloch and the Meaning of the Augustan Census Figures," *Journal of Roman Studies* 84 (1994) 23-40, where another estimate pushes this higher even around 28 BCE, and Neville Morley, *Metropolis and Hinterland: The City of Rome and the Italian Economy 200 B.C. – A.D. 200.* Cambridge: Cambridge University Press, 1996, 182; cf. Walter Scheidel, "Roman population size: the logic of the debate," *Princeton - Stanford Working Papers in Classics 2.0.* Princeton, NJ, 2007. Scheidel infers a 800,000 - 1,000,000 "metropolitan" population in 28 BCE, p. 10 footnote 46 and p. 11. (https://www.princeton.edu/~pswpc/pdfs/scheidel/070706.pdf).

4   J. J. Walsh, *The Great Fire of Rome: Life and Death in the Ancient City.* Baltimore: Johns Hopkins University Press, 2019, 38, 50. Walsh describes the flammability of Rome's wooden old inner city and mentions how many different historical periods constructed overlying structures on the "rubble and corpses" of earlier layered buildings.

5   Wilhelmina Jashemski and F. G. Meyer, eds., *The Natural History of Pompeii.* Cambridge: Cambridge University Press, 2002, esp. 4-5, 217-239 (various chapters of burnt wood remains alone by P. Hatcher, S. T. Mols and P. Kuniholm including dendrochronology

in the latter); Patrick Hunt, "Pompeii" in *Ten Discoveries That Rewrote History*, ch. 6. New York: Penguin Group, 2007, 111.

6   Chad Emmett, "The Capital Cities of Jerusalem," *Geographical Review* 86.2 (1996), 233-58, esp. 233.

7   This conservative date range (970-31 BCE) assumes the accuracy of Egyptian records of Pharaoh Shishak (Sheshonq) claiming he invaded Judah and thereby humiliated Rehoboam, Solomon's son around 926 BCE five years into his reign, and also the accuracy of the biblical narrative of Solomonic succession to Rehoboam after a putative reign of 40 years (I Kings 11:42).

8   Barry Weiss, "The Decline of Late Bronze Age Civilization as a Possible Response to Climatic Change," *Climate Change* 4.2 (1982), 173-98; Guy D. Middleton, "Nothing Lasts Forever: Environmental Discourses on the collapse of Past Societies," *Journal of Archaeological Research* 20 (2012), 257-307.

9   Marc van der Mieroop, *A History of the Ancient Near East ca. 3000-323 BC.* Oxford: Blackwell, 2006, 190.

10 James Monson, *The Land Between: A Regional Study Guide to the Land of the Bible.* Jerusalem: Biblical Backgrounds, 1996, 12-13, 280-1; A. H. Joffe, "The Rise of Secondary States in the Iron Age Levant," *Journal of the Economic and Social History of the Orient* 45.4 (2002), 425-67. The normal zenith back and forth of empires controlling the Levant usually saw either Egypt or Mesopotamia dominant; at times it could also be an Anatolian power from the north especially in the Late Bronze Age from the Hittites, but between Late Bronze and Early Iron the zenith of the Hittites passed and their old empire was broken.

11 Eric Cline, *1177 BC: The Year Civilization Collapsed.* Princeton: Princeton University Press, 2015, 2,9; A. Bernard Knapp and Sturt Manning, "Crisis in Context: the End of the Late Bronze Age in the Eastern Mediterranean," *American Journal of Archaeology* 120.1 (2016), 99-149.

12 M. Liverani, "The collapse of the Near Eastern regional system at the end of the Bronze Age: the case of Syria," in *Centre and Periphery in the Ancient World*, M. Rowlands, M. T. Larsen, K. Kristiansen, eds. Cambridge: Cambridge University Press, 1987.

13 Elizabeth Knott, "The Middle Babylonian / Kassite Period (ca. 1595–1155 B.C.) in Mesopotamia," *Heilbrunn Timeline of Art History*. New York: The Metropolitan Museum of Art, 2000–. http://www.metmuseum.org/toah/hd/kass/hd_kass.htm (June 2016); "Assyria, 1365–609 B.C." Department of Ancient Near Eastern Art. In *Heilbrunn Timeline of Art History*. New York: The Metropolitan Museum of Art, 2000–. http://www.metmuseum.org/toah/hd/assy/hd_assy.htm (originally published October 2004, last revised April 2010).

14 Robert Drews, *The End of the Bronze Age: Changes in Warfare and the Catastrophe ca. 1200 BC*. Princeton: Princeton University Press, 1993; Cline, xvii.

15 Monson, *The Land Between*, e.g., 13-14, 25, 27, 34-37, 64-65, esp. 36 & 280.

16 Philip J. King, "Travel, Transport, Trade," *Eretz-Israel* 26 (1999) Israel Exploration Society, 94-105. Gaza to Jerusalem to the Jordan Valley and the Transjordanian King's Highway was a known route along with the central north-south hill route; Monson, 60, 64.

17 Quintus Curtius Rufus, *History of Alexander* 5.11, noting Arabia as famous for perfumes. Frankincense mostly came from the extreme tip of the Southern Arabian peninsula, myrrh as well from Arabia. Gus van Beek. "Frankincense and Myrrh," *Biblical Archaeologist* 23.3 (1960) 69-95; G. Lankester Harding, "The Story of Frankincense," *Saudi Aramco World*, Jan/Feb, 1965, 24-27; Middle East Institute, 2019 (mei.edu); Daniel Master, "Economy and Exchange in the Iron Age Kingdoms of the Southern Levant," *Bulletin of the American Schools of Oriental Research* (BASOR) 372 (2014), 81-97; Gunnar Sperveslage, "Intercultural Contacts between Egypt and the Arabian Peninsula at the turn off the 2nd to 1st millennium BCE," in *Dynamics of Production in the Ancient Near East: 1300– 500 BC*. J.

C. Moreno Garcia, ed. Oxford: Oxbow Books, 2016, ch. 14 about frankincense, myrrh and other spices. Cumin appears in Deir el-Medina, New Kingdom Egypt, 18th Dynasty (ended in 1292 BCE). Also see Patrick Hunt, "Plant Technology and Science in Antiquity (Plant Perfume Use and Technology in Antiquity)" in Annette L. Giesecke, ed. *Bloomsbury Cultural History of Plants*, ch. 4, Section 4, vol. 1, Antiquity, London: Bloomsbury, forthcoming, 2021.

18 *Mycenaean Linear B Glossary,* University of New Mexico, 6 (www.unm.edu/~blanter/Linear_B_Glossary.pdf).

19 Patrick Hunt, "Sensory Images in the Song of Songs." [Collected Papers of the IOSOT Congress, Paris, Sorbonne-College de France]. *Beitrage zur Erforhschung des Alten Testaments und des Antiken Judentums*, Band 28 (1996) 188-94; Patrick Hunt, *Poetry in the Song of Songs: A Literary Analysis.* Studies in Biblical Literature 96. Frankfurt: Peter Lang Verlag, 2008, ch. 5, esp. 105 as well as 103-09, 115-30.

20 Nathan Katz, "From Legend to History: India and Israel in the Ancient World," *Shofar: Interdisciplinary Journal of Jewish Studies* 17.3 (Special Issue: Judaism and Asian Religions) (1999), 7-22; Richard Foltz, "Judaism and the Silk Route," *The History Teacher: Society for History Education* 32.1 (1998), 9-16.

21 Roger Nam, *Portrayals of Economic Exchange in the Book of Kings.* Leiden: E. J. Brill, 2012, 181 & ff. Also see Susan and Andrew Sherratt, "The Growth of the Mediterranean Economy in the Early First Millennium BC," *World Archaeology* 24.3 (1993), 361-78.

22 Thomas Levy et al., "High-precision radiocarbon dating and historical biblical archaeology in southern Jordan," *Proceedings of the National Academy of Science* 105 [43] October 28, 2008, 16460-16465.

23 "King Solomon's Copper Mines?" *Science Daily* October 28, 2008 (https://www.sciencedaily.com/releases/2008/10/081027174545.htm).

24 "Expedition Claims Evidence of Queen of Sheba Found in Ethiopia,"
    Biblical Archaeology Society News. Feb 14, 2012 (https://www.bib-
    licalarchaeology.org/daily/news/expedition-claims-evidence-of-
    queen-of-sheba-found-in-ethiopia/); Stanley Stewart. "In Search of
    the Real Queen of Sheba." *National Geographic News,* Dec. 3, 2018
    (https://www.nationalgeographic.com/travel/destinations/africa/
    ethiopia/mysterious-queen-sheba-legend-church-archaeology/)

25 A. Mazar, *Excavations at Tell Qasile, Part Two. Various Finds, The
    Pottery, Conclusions, Appendices* (*Qedem* 20). Jerusalem: The Hebrew
    University of Jerusalem 1985; Archaeological Sites No. 8. "Tel
    Qasile—A Philistine Settlement with a Temple," *Israeli Ministry
    of Foreign Affairs,* Nov. 26, 2003. (https://mfa.gov.il/mfa/israelex-
    perience/history/pages/tel%20qasile%20-%20a%20philistine%20
    settlement%20with%20a%20temple.aspx)

26 W. B. Hafford, "Mesopotamian Mensuration Balance Pan Weights
    from Nippur," *Journal of the Economic and Social History of the
    Orient* 48.3 (2005), 345-87.

27 M. Siani-Davies, "Ptolemy XII Auletes and the Romans," *Historia:
    Zeitschrift für Alte Geschichte* Bd. 46. H. 3,3 (1997), 306-40.

28 Richard Westall, "The Loan to Ptolemy XII, 59-48 BCE," *Ricerche di
    Egittologia e di Antichità Copte* (*REAC* 12) (2010), 25.

29 In addition to Herodotus, *History* III.89-95, Borza maintained
    Darius carried millions of pounds of gold and silver across his
    empire in moving his winter to summer capitals. Eugene N. Borza,
    "Fire From Heaven: Alexander at Persepolis," *Classical Philology*
    67.4 (1972), 233-45.

30 Millard, 1989, 22-3; Kitchen, 1989, 30.

31 According N. G. L. Hammond, *Sources for Alexander the Great.*
    Cambridge: Cambridge University Press, 1993, 67ff. Justin (*Epitome
    of Pompeius Trogus* 11.14.8) is the source for Alexander's 40,000 tal-
    ents of precious metals captured at Susa, not necessarily credible.

32 Pauline Albenda, *The Palace of Sargon, King of Assyria: Monumental Wall Reliefs at Dur-Sharrukin* (from original drawings made at the time of their discovery in 1843–1844 by Botta and Flandin). Paris: Éditions Recherche sur les civilisations, 1986, esp. 91, 110 & Plate 133; Pauline Albenda, "Dur-Shurrakin, the Royal City of Sargon II, King of Assyria," *Bulletin: Canadian Society for Mesopotamian Studies* 38 (2003), 5-13. In her 2003 survey Albenda describes Flandin's ca. 1844 illustrations of the material Botta excavated, much lost in the Tigris near Basra en route to Paris, some also preserved in the Louvre, 8.

33 D. D. Luckenbill, *Ancient Records of Assyria and Babylon*, vol. 2. Oriental Institute Chicago: University of Chicago Press, 1927, 211 [527] & 228-9 [583-85], These accounts are from Esharhaddon's Prism A (British Museum) and the Dog River Stele found near Beirut.

34 In J. B. Pritchard, ed., *Ancient Near Eastern Texts*. Princeton: Princeton University Press, 1969, 3rd ed., 280.

35 Quirke and Spencer, 47.

36 Kitchen, 1989, 30.

37 The Bubastite Portal—not comprehensive due to lacunae and inscriptions destroyed—recording Shishak's campaign "itinerary" is divided up into several Levant sections by region, with the place names given in rows. For the Coastal Plain, Shephelah, Meggido and Jezreel Plain regions: Row 2, on (#20) is destroyed; Row 3, one (#30) is incomplete with lacunae; much worse is Row 4 where quite a few names are destroyed (#42-44 & #48-50, 52) for a total of 7 out of 13 place names) and quite a few are incomplete (#41, 45-6, 51) are incomplete with one (#47) illegible (a total of 5 out of 13), so only 1 place name out of 13 is actually legible in Row 4, although unidentified; Row 5, several names (#62-3) are destroyed and several (#60, 61 and 64) are too incomplete to be conclusive, as 5 out of 13 illegible; Row 6 on the Negev region, Row 6, 3 names (#79-82) are incomplete and therefore illegible; Row 7 has a few

incomplete (#91, 98); Row 8 has a few destroyed (#114-115) and a few incomplete (#102, 105, 113, 116) and only 5 of 13 are identified; Row 9, at least 8 names are incomplete (#117-120, 129-32) and only 5 of 13 are identified; Row 10 names are mostly destroyed (#134-38, 141, 143-44, 147-48) for a total of 10 destroyed and 4 incomplete (#142, 145, 146, 149) so that only 2 names out of 13 are even identified. Row 10 84-91extension has 5 names with only 2 identified. As mentioned, a total of only 52 or around a third of the 156 place names are reliably identified with at least 22 place names destroyed and at least 30 incomplete or illegible with at least 34 unidentified.

38 Pritchard, 1969 ed., 263-4.

39 T. L. Sagrillo, "Šišak's army: 2 Chronicle 12:2-3," in *Culture and History, Proceedings of the Int'l. Conference, University of Haifa May 2-5 2010.* Münster: Ugarit-Verlag, 425-50; Israel Finkelstein. "The Last Labayu: King Saul and the Expansion of the First North Israelite Territorial Entity," in Yairah Amit, Ehud Ben Zvi, Israel Finkelstein, et al., eds. *Essays on Ancient Israel in Its Near Eastern Context: A Tribute to Nadav Na'aman.* Winona Lake: Eisenbrauns, 2006. 171 & ff.

40 Jane Cahill, "Jerusalem in David's and Solomon's Time," *Biblical Archaeology Review* 30.6 (2004); Eilat Mazar, "Did I Find King David's Palace?" *Biblical Archaeology Review* 32.1 (2006); Yosef Garfinkal and Saar Ganor, *Khirbet Qeiyafa Vol. 1. The 2007-2008 Excavation seasons.* Jerusalem: Israel Exploration Society, 2009; Jonathan Tubb, "Editorial: Early Iron Age Judah in the Light of Recent Discoveries at Khirbet Qeiyafa," *Palestine Exploration Quarterly* 142 (2009), 1-2; Daniel Pioske, "David's Jerusalem: A Sense of Place," *Near Eastern Archaeology* 76.1 (2013), 4-15; Yosef Garfinkal, Saar Ganor, Michael G. Hasel, *Khirbet Qeiyafa Vol. 2. Excavation Report 2009-2013: Stratigraphy and Architecture (Areas B, C, D, E).* Jerusalem: Israel Exploration Society, 2014; Y. Garfinkel and M. Mumcuoglu, *Solomon's Temple and Palace:*

New Archaeological Discoveries. Jerusalem: Korn (Hebrew), 2015; Katharina Galor, *Finding Jerusalem: Archaeology Between Science and Ideology.* Berkeley: University of California Press, 2017.

Although the debate about David and Solomonic Jerusalem is not without detractors for Davidic Jerusalem: see Israel Finkelstein, "The 'Large Stone Structure' in Jerusalem: Reality vs. Yearning," *Zeitschrift des Deutschen Palästina Vereins* 127 (2011), 1-11. Yet also note the much earlier article by Kathleen Kenyon, "Ancient Jerusalem," *Scientific American* 213.1 (1965), 84-91, where she acknowledges archaeological traces for the small Davidic city ca. 1000 BCE supplanting the Jebusite stronghold.

41 K.A. Kitchen, *On the Reliability of the Old Testament.* Grand Rapids: William B. Eerdmans & Co, 2003, 10, 32–34, 607 (image with Shishak's cartouche).

42 Taylor Cylinder Prism, British Museum # 91032, Column II line 37—Column III line 49; Luckenbill, *AR II*, 1927, §240, 121.

43 Rassam Cylinder Prism, British Museum # 91026, after 3rd campaign, lines 20-33; Luckenbill, *AR II*, 1927, §284, 136.

44 British Museum # 21946 (Cuneiform Tablet) *ABC* [*Assyrian and Babylonian Chronicles*] 5: Nebuchadnezzar's Jerusalem Conquest; A. K. Grayson, *Assyrian and Babylonian Chronicles.* Locust Valley, NY: J. J. Augustin, 1975 (Winona Lake, IN: Eisenbrauns, 2000).

5

Paleopathology and the Destruction of Sennacherib's Army Besieging Jerusalem in II Chronicles 32 and II Kings 19

❖

Peter Paul Rubens, The Defeat of Sennacherib, ca.1612-14,
Alte Pinakothek, Munich (Image in public domain)

Historians know disease often stalks armies in history.[1] The specter of invisible pathogens haunting ancient warfare may have at times seemed instead like a punitive deity taking sides.

Sometimes it's merely a much simpler question of contagion and the inability to protect against it.

While there is insufficient documentation to sort out this question in the biblical narratives of II Chronicles 32, II Kings 18-20, and Isaiah 22 & 36, these texts dovetail variously in the siege of Jerusalem by the Assyrian king Sennacherib, especially in the invasion preparations of the Judean king Hezekiah and the massive death toll experienced by Sennacherib as recorded in these biblical passages. The account of many thousands of soldiers suddenly dying in one night by the hand of the "Angel of the Lord" appears to be supernatural hyperbole, but perhaps there is also a more natural explanation for the sudden catastrophic demise of an invading force. While we have no epidemiological evidence for this event, these literary texts of II Chronicles 32 and II Kings 18 may reveal some compelling suggestions for what easily may have happened.

Comparisons may be found readily elsewhere. Historical biopsy aside, the Assyrian invasion and siege of Jerusalem datable to 701 BCE wouldn't be the first or last time a wartime population was decimated by plague or disease, as Thucydides recounts in 430 BCE (although plague returned several times in the ensuing few years) with the movements of armies:

> Not many days after their arrival in Attica the plague first began to show itself among the Athenians. It was said that it had broken out in many places previously in the neighborhood of Lemnos and elsewhere; but a pestilence of such extent and mortality was nowhere remembered. Neither were the physicians at first of any service, ignorant as they were of the proper way to treat it, but they died themselves the most thickly, as they visited the sick most often; nor did any human art succeed any better. Supplications in the temples, divinations, and so forth were found equally futile, till the overwhelming nature of the disaster at last put a stop to them altogether....All the birds and beasts that prey upon human bodies, either abstained from touching them

(though there were many lying unburied), or died after tasting them. In proof of this, it was noticed that birds of this kind actually disappeared; they were not about the bodies, or indeed to be seen at all....the catastrophe was so overwhelming that men, not knowing what would happen next to them, became indifferent to every rule of religion or law.[2]

M. Sweerts, Ancient Plague of Athens, ca. 1653, LACMA
(Image in public domain)

Although the debate continues regarding the exact agent of plague that struck Athens (with archaeological evidence of sudden mass graves of at least 1000 people), there is little argument that it was pandemic. At least one historian has addressed such events: "Infectious diseases put an end to the Golden Age of Athens, wrecked Justinian's dream of restoring the Roman Empire to its former glory."[3]

According to both II Chronicles 32:5, and Isaiah 22:10, Hezekiah prepared for the Assyrian invasion by multiple actions, including strengthening the walls of Jerusalem—at least one wall has been found and securely dated by archaeological research and now known as "Avigad's Wall" (visited by the author in 1984 and still visible in the Jewish Quarter).[4] Related in II Chronicles 32:3-4, II Kings 20 and Isaiah 22:11, Hezekiah also took proactive hydrological measures to restrict Assyrian access to flowing water by blocking the flowing springs external to the city and also cutting a rock conduit underground that collected the water resources within the city. Known today as the "Siloam Tunnel" (which this author also walked through from the Gihon Spring to the Siloam Pool in 1985) and arguably dated (note the claims and counterclaims in the footnote here) by its inscription ostensibly to the end of the 8th c. BCE in Hezekiah's time,[5] this limestone channel protected the city by keeping the Gihon spring from flowing out into the

N. Avigad, "Hezekiah's Wall, 1970 (Photo P. Hunt)

Kidron Valley and instead brought it back underground through the limestone into the lower city now safely within the new wall.

Blocking the springs around Jerusalem—possibly by a mass effort of filling up with rocks and soil—would create a huge water crisis for the Assyrian invading force besieging the city, because, as noted in II Chronicles 32:3-4, armies needed a consistent large drinking source for themselves and their animals:

> He [Hezekiah] planned with his officers and his warriors to stop the flow of the springs that were outside the city; and they helped him. A great many people were gathered, and they stopped all the springs and the stream that flowed through the land, saying, "Why should the Assyrian kings come and find water in abundance?"

Limiting access to fresh water would be advantageous for the city under siege (especially if their own water sources were protected as noted above) and extremely disadvantageous for the invaders the longer a siege lasted. If sufficient water could not be obtained or whatever limited water was contaminated, the specter of dehydration and pathogens is multiplied immensely. One such agent of plague death (a metaphor for "the Angel of the Lord"?) is the known vector of rapidly multiplying cholera spread by the bacteria *Vibrio cholera* through infected water, especially if rehydration with fresh water was not possible for the same reason of blocked water sources.

Siloam Tunnel (Image in public domain)

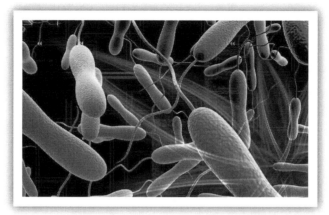

Vibrio cholera (Image in public domain)

When good, clean water is not easily available, after drinking fecally-contaminated water, large demographic sectors for centuries across the world—recorded in urban London, India, China, among others—have been quickly incapacited and often decimated as cholera can kill within hours of contamination if untreated. This is confirmed in modern accounts from both the 19th through 20th and 21st centuries in wartime contamination.[6] According to the Mayo Clinic, cholera causes severe dehydration with up to 6.33 gallons (24 liters) of water loss per diem—or water loss of a liter per hour—with a following drop in blood pressure and debilitating cramps. Critical mass bacterial incubation after exposure can be as quick as 12 hours.[7] Typically cholera morbidity in modern times has been estimated at 20% of infected hosts but can be much higher depending on cramped quarters, shared water and food resources, lack of hygiene and no remediation.[8] The II Kings 19:35 account specifies 185,000 Assyrians died that night whereas the II Chronicles 32:21 account merely notes massive deaths of the army: "The LORD sent an angel who cut off all the mighty warriors, commanders and officers in the camp of the king of Assyria."

For an extra-biblical account, Sennacherib's Prism (Oriental Institute, Chicago, also British Museum copy) doesn't record the death of his army but merely that his siege of Jerusalem was unsuccessful

Oriental Institute Chicago   *British Museum, London*

Sennacherib Prism
(Left photo, Image in public domain; Right photo, P. Hunt)

by extrapolation: he does not claim victory but only that he "shut up Hezekiah like a bird in a cage."

While this author is not the first to connect pathogens and especially cholera to this Sennacherib invasion event of 701 BCE,[9] his ample development of the idea here follows his other paleopathology discussion(s) of ancient world army decimation.[10] However conjectural, assuming the biblical accounts are recording actual events—certainly not contradicted by the Assyrian cuneiform versions including Sennacherib's Prism—cholera or a similar pathogen makes immediate sense as the natural background for the "supernatural" decimation of Sennacherib's army and subsequent return to Nineveh without a successful siege of Jerusalem.

❖

Endnotes Chapter 5

1   Bernard Rostker, *Providing for the Casualties of War*, Rand Corporation, 2013, ch. 9, 241: "From the time of the Greeks...just being a soldier was an open invitation to death from the countless communicable diseases that were the scourge of military camps."

2   Thucydides, *Peloponnesian War*, 2.47.3-4, 50.1, 52.3

3   R. S. Bray, *Armies of Pestilence: The Impact of Disease on History.* Barnes and Noble reprint, 1996, intro. Also see William Rosen, *Justinian's Flea: The First Great Plague and the End of the Roman Empire*, Penguin, 2008, for a popular application of the Constantinople plague information provided by Procopius in his *Secet History.* mid-6th c. CE.

4   M. Broshi, "The Expansion of Jerusalem in the Reigns of Hezekiah and Manessah," *Israel Exploration Journal* 24.1 (1974), 21-6, note p. 21.

5   A. E. Shimron and A. Frumkin, "The Why How and When of the Siloam Tunnel Reevaluated: A Reply," *Bulletin of the American Schools of Oriental Research* 364 (2011) 53-60 (this article challenges the geology of the Sneh, Weinberger, and Shalev article of the same name and same journal (*BASOR* 359 of 2010); G. A. Rendsburg and W. M. Schniedewind, "The Siloam Tunnel Inscription: Historical and Linguistic Perspectives," *Israel Exploration Journal 60 (2010) 188-203* (note the more compelling arguments for it being Hezekiah's construction); M. K. Y. H. Hom. "Where Art Thou, O Hezekiah's Tunnel...[Waterworks]," *Journal of Biblical Literature* 135.3 (2016), 493-503. Note in above Rendsburg and Schniedewind 2010 citation, footnote 1, p. 188: "While there is no absolute proof that the Siloam Tunnel is the tunnel attributed to King Hezekiah in the biblical sources, with no evidence to the contrary (especially in light of other studies cited herein), our standpoint is that they are one and the same."

6   J. Glenn Morris, "Cholera: Modern Pandemic Disease of Ancient Lineage," *Emerging Infectious Diseases* vol. 17 (11) November, 2011, 2099-2104; "Cholera: Key Facts," *World Health Organization* January 17, 2019 (https://www.who.int/news-room/fact-sheets/detail/cholera).

7   Remy Melina, "How Does Cholera Kill?" Live Science, October 22, 2010, quoting Mayo Clinic staff and Jason Harris, Massachusetts General Hospital, (https://www.livescience.com/10212-cholera-kill.html).

8   E. J. Nelson, J. B. Harris, J. Glenn Morris, S. B. Calderwood, A. Camilli. "Cholera Transmission: the Host, pathogen and bacterio-phage dynamic," *Nature Reviews Microbiology* 7 (2009), 693-702 (https://www.ncbi.nlm.nih.gov/pmc/articles/PMC3842031/); E. K. Lipp, A. Huq, R. R. Colwell, "Effects of global climate on in factious disease: the cholera model," *Clinical Microbiology Reviews* 15.4 (2002), 757-70 (https://www.ncbi.nlm.nih.gov/pubmed/12364378/).

9   In his *New Oxford Annotated Bible* commentary p. 566 on II *Kings* 19:35-36, Iain Provan notes "some commentators suggest that nature causes, such as plague, may lie behind the reference to the action of the *angel of the* LORD." The "angel of the LORD" also reminds of the plague of the first-born in Egypt in *Exodus* 12:29-30 although there it is the LORD as agent of death. Note John Bright, *A History of Israel,* Westminster/John Knox Press, 2000 ed., 24 & ff. discusses plague in this event as does eminent historian William H. Macneill in his essay in the collection *What If?* (*The World's Foremost Military Historians Imagine What Might Have Been*) G. P. Putnam's Sons, 1999.

10   Patrick Hunt and Andreaa Seicean, "Alpine Archaeology and Paleopathology: Was Hannibal's Army also decimated by epidemic while crossing the Alps?" *Archaeolog* (Stanford) May 20, 2007. https://web.stanford.edu/dept/archaeology/cgi-bin/archaeolog/?p=123.

6

Gehenna: Hell as Metaphor? What and Where was It?

❖

Hell, detail in Pieter Bruegel the Elder's Dull Griet, 1561
(Photo P. Hunt)

*G*ehenna is an old Hebrew toponym (place name) that began as a literal, physical location—the Valley of Hinnom—and gradually transformed into a metaphor for hell through various processes including religious defilement. One of the immediate problems of any hermeneutics about Gehenna is the religious literariness of the narrative texts and subsequent metaphorical language therein right up through the Roman period rather than the verifiable knowledge of what can be documented as having happened in an otherwise-known topographic place.

As mentioned in Hebrew biblical texts, this valley just south of ancient Jerusalem was carved by a stream that joined the Kidron Valley. Today the valley marks the limits of Old Jerusalem outside the late medieval Suleimanic Wall—itself roughly paralleling older walls from the Iron Age of the first millennium BCE into Roman times—surrounding Mt. Zion, its southeastern confluence with the south running Kidron Valley is near where the Tyrollean Valley (or *Maqtesh*) descends out of the summit of Old Jerusalem and also where the Kidron had continued southerly under the Ophel or Hill of David. Perhaps ironically, the depth of the Hinnom Valley, so accursed in literature, is immediately adjacent to the blessed context of the height of Mt. Zion. This polarity of sublime blessed height to terrible depth has not been missed by commentators. While some dispute, however, the exact location of its defiling activity of child sacrifice or that such even occurred, all agree the Hinnom Valley was immediately south of Old Jeruslaem's walls. Notice on the map below that the Hinnom Valley runs eastward south of the city walls.

Named after the Son of Hinnom, the Valley Ben-Hinnom (גֵּי בֶן־הִנֹּם) is first mentioned in Joshua 15 circumscribing the boundary of the tribe of Judah near the then-Canaanite fortress of Jebus that would become the core of the site of the city of Jerusalem: "Then it ran up the Valley of Ben Hinnom along the southern slope of the Jebusite city. From there it climbed to the top of the hill west of the Hinnom Valley." [NIV]

The Jebusites were apparently conquered in the Davidic period (most likely 11th c. BCE) and Jebus on the Ophel became Jerusalem during the time of David. Political prescience is involved in the choice of the capital of Israel for at least two reasons: First, Jerusalem was located in the small tribe of Benjamin, which served as a buffer state between the two powerful tribes of Ephraim to the north and Judah to the south, both of which jockeyed for supremacy in Israel.[1] Second, trade routes from east to west converged here from the Jordan to the Mediterranean coast, so this location for a capital was pragmatic. At the time of conquest, the Hinnom Valley was unimportant other than as a boundary marker.

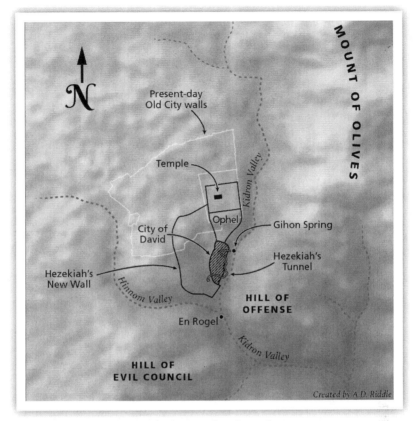

Hezekiah's Jerusalem, late 8th c. BCE

According to Jeremiah 7:30-33, the eternal curse on the Hinnom Valley is due to Judahite idolatry around the 8th-7th c. BCE borrowed from Canaanite and Phoenician religion and connected to the attendant human sacrifice that purportedly occurred there in what is usually called a *tophet* or funerary sanctuary to the gods Tanit and Ba'al as her consort, as found in Phoenician-Punic Carthage, Phoenician Motya off Sicily, and Tharros in Sardinia, among others,[2] although this human sacrificial designation also is often disputed as merely a circular argument from biblical sources. As Jeremiah 7:30-33 relates:

> "…They have set up their detestable idols in the house that bears my Name and have defiled it. They have built the high

places of Tophet (תּוֹפֶת) in the Valley of Ben Hinnom to burn their sons and daughters in the fire—something I did not command, nor did it enter my mind. So beware, the days are coming, declares the Lord, when people will no longer call it Tophet (תּוֹפֶת) or the Valley of Ben Hinnom, but the Valley of Slaughter, for they will bury the dead in Tophet until there is no more room. Then the carcasses of this people will become food for the birds and the wild animals, and there will be no one to frighten them away." [NIV]

The word *tophet* (Hebrew feminine singular) itself is a funerary word as a cognate of other similar Indo-European words, among them *taphos* as "grave" in Greek, hence the modern word "epitaph" (from *epi* + *taphos*) for a grave marker inscription. Archaeology refers to the general study of grave contexts and things found—grave goods—therein as taphonomics.

Hieronymus Bosch. "Hell" in *The Garden of Earthly Delights*
ca. 1490-1510. Prado Museum, Madrid (Photo P. Hunt)

As mentioned, the most famous (or infamous) tophet is that of the sacred precinct of Tanit in Carthage, excavated in the 1980s by Harvard Semitic Museum under Lawrence Stager and Sam Wolff,[3] also visited and researched by this author funded by National Geographic for his *Hannibal* book.[4] Their findings are controversial because not all agree it was a locus of normative infant sacrifice. Nevertheless, the practice was also documented, however propagandistically, by Diodorus Siculus (1st c. BCE) where among other details he describes the quantities of children sacrificed by the general populace in his *Bibliotheke History* XX. 6-7.[5] At the Carthage Tophet, at least 3000 burial urns of children and animal ash and bones are documented over hundreds of years through multiple strata.[6] Naturally this is a contentious subject and some scholars disagree with both the premise of child sacrifice and/or that it might ever have been normative behavior in Carthage.[7] (Again, see author's notes in Hannibal, pp. 9 and 277 for longer discussion.) On the other hand, David Soren et al. document that even after 146 BCE

Carthage: Tophet of Tanit Sanctuary (Photo in public domain)

when Rome conquered Carthage that the "ancient rites of child sacrifice continued in the hinterland right into late antiquity, although offerings such as the first fruits of the season, birds, and animals such as rams or goats were more common."[8]

Israelite religion forbade sacrifice to *Molech*, the "ruler (מֶלֶךְ) [of live sacrifice]" as seen in *Leviticus* 18:21 and elsewhere: "And thou shalt not let any of thy seed pass through the fire to Molech (מֹלֶךְ), neither shalt thou profane the name of thy God: I am the LORD."

Other Hebrew scriptures such as II *Kings* 23:10 continue this description in the reforms of King Josiah: "And he defiled Tophet (תֹּפֶת), which is in the valley of the children of Hinnom, that no man might make his son or his daughter to pass through the fire to Moloch (מֹלֶךְ)."

Jeremiah 32:35 provides additional detail: "And they built the high places of Ba'al, which are in the valley of the son of Hinnom, to cause their sons and their daughters to pass through the fire unto Molech (מֹלֶךְ) which I commanded them not, neither came it into my mind, that they should do this abomination, to cause Judah to sin."

Thus, *Molech* as used in the biblical texts is generally suggested as a title for Ba'al and/or his consort Tanit as the "ruler" (מֹלֶךְ *Molech)* [of live sacrifice]." Judaism's mixed record of the Hinnom Valley as a *tophet* notwithstanding, its notoriety accrued through the attested connection with King Manasseh, Hezekiah's son, who was said to cause his children to pass through the fire ostensibly there in II Kings 21:6 and amplified in II Chronicles 33:6 to include the exact location as the Hinnom Valley:

"And he made his son to pass through the fire…"

"He also made his children to pass through the fire in the valley of the son of Hinnom (בְּגֵי-בֶן-הִנֹּם)."

So, nearly every subsequent mention of the Valley of Hinnom makes it clear that it was the locus of apparent human sacrifice to foreign (= false) gods in Hebrew religious perception, and was thus accursed because of this abominable practice.

Because the subsequent Aramaization of *Ge-Hinnom* (גֵּי-הִנֹּם) becomes *Gehenna* and also because the Septuagint and Hellenization of

Gehenna becomes Γέεννα in Koine Greek, this latter Greek word is used multiple times in the New Testament Gospels, especially in the narratives of Jesus. For example, seven passages in Matthew (5:22, 29, 30; 10:28; 18:9; 23:15; 23:33), three in Mark (9:43, 45, 47) and one in Luke (12:5) all mention *Gehenna* (Γέεννα in Greek) as a place of torment and perishing. Matthew 10:28 mentions *Gehenna* (Γέεννα in Greek) as a place of destruction for both body and soul and Mark 9:43 identifies it as a topos of "unquenchable fire". How much of the polemic of Jesus is metaphor and how much is a description of "Hell" is impossible to ascertain. It has been duly noted that the multiplicity of explicit mentions of *Gehenna* by Jesus make it seem like a real place and not merely a figurative idea or metaphor.

Nonetheless, despite the details of II Kings 21 & 23 and II Chronicles 33 noting Manasseh's sins and Josiah's reforms and the judgments of Jeremiah (chs. 7, 32) the archaeological evidence for the Hinnom Valley as a topos for a Molech shrine of child sacrifice—or a perpetually-burning trash dump in the time of Jesus—is so scanty as to be unverifiable to date. It should be noted, however, as some have, that Josiah's reforms purportedly would have desecrated the Molech shrines and thus any such evidence might have been destroyed at this time.

Whether the Hinnom Valley was used in Roman times as a trash dump with smoking embers—and thus a literal suggestion by Jesus—remains elusive. Despite long but sporadic Rabbinic tradition (Rabbi Yohanan ben Zakkai, Rabbi Jeremiah ben Eleazar, among others) and extended commentary for apocryphal *Book of Enoch* xxvii.1 as noted in the *Jewish Encyclopedia* where *Gehenna*, and possibly by extension the accursed Hinnom Valley, became "a figurative equivalent for hell"[9] and specifically Rabbi David Kimhi claiming a trash dump in the Hinnom Valley, Lloyd Bailey states that "There is no evidence that the valley was, in fact, a garbage dump…"[10] Trash dumps for burning by fire in Jerusalem would be logical south, east and southeast of the city where acrid smoke would blow away from occupation areas. A contemporary 1st c. BCE to 1st c. CE Roman trash dump can be seen to the east in the Kidron valley with many accumulated strata of compacted refuse material,[11] but without obvious ash deposits that would

Y. Gadot, Kidron's Jerusalem Landfill of 1st c CE (Courtesy BAS)

evidence burning of refuse. If Roman period burning trash dumps were observed by Jesus to elicit such a metaphor, they have yet to be archaeologically proven.

In conclusion, since millennia of alluviation and modern redevelopment in the vicinity has made the Hinnom Valley increasingly difficult to pinpoint any such locus for the kind of activity II Kings, II Chronicles and Jeremiah narrate, complicated by the lack of physical evidence for a Roman period trash dump there to date, the words of Jesus must be at this point figurative. It cannot be fully ruled out that Jesus was describing a real place. Perhaps extended future archaeological research will yet locate a Hinnom Valley trash dump whose "unquenchable fire" was known and its acrid smoke seen and smelled by Jerusalemites of the Roman period including Jesus who referenced an accursed place to avoid if at all possible.

❖

Endnotes Chapter 6

1   James W. Flanagan, "The Relocation of the Davidic Capital," *Journal of the American Academy of Religion* 47.2 1979, 223-44.

2   Other Phoenician Tanit sanctuaries or *tophets* are found at Sulcis, Bithia, and Nora, all on Sardinia.

3   Richard Clifford, "Phoenician Religion," in *Bulletin of the American Society of Oriental Religion (BASOR)* 279 (1990), 55-64; Lawrence E. Stager, "The Rite of Child Sacrifice at Carthage," in J. G. Pedley, *New Light on Ancient Carthage,* University of Michigan Press, 1990, 1-11; L. E. Stager, "A View from the Tophet," in *Phönizer im Westen,* Philip von Zabern, 1982, 155-66.

4   Patrick Hunt, *Hannibal,* Simon and Schuster, 2017, Ch. 1, 9-10, note 12, 276-77.

5   *Bibliotheke Historia* XX.6-7 (*Library of History*: "…In their zeal to make amends for their omission, they selected two hundred of the noblest children and sacrificed them publicly; and others who were under suspicion sacrificed themselves voluntarily, in number not less than three hundred").

6   L. Stager and S. Wolff, "Child sacrifice at Carthage: Religious Rite for Population Control?" *Biblical Archaeology Review* 10 (1984), 30-51. Co-author Sam Wolff confirmed in London at the Institute of Archaeology (pers. comm.) that they only excavated 10% of the Tanit Sanctuary Tophet and suggested that this limited number of 3000 urns with multiple burnt burials could exceed an exponential number of burials—up to 30,000?—if the full precinct were to be excavated. Also note P. Smith, G. Avishai, J. A. Greene and L. E. Stager, "Aging Cremated Infants: the Problem of Sacrifice at the Tophet of Carthage," *Antiquity* 85 (2011), 859-74.

7   Jeffrey Schwartz, Frank Houghton, Roberto Machiarelli and Luca Bondioli, "Skeletal Remains from Punic Carthage Do Not Support Systematic Sacrifice of Infants," *PLoS (Public Library of Science)* 5,

2, (February 17, 2010), e9177. Yet note more recent arguments for Phoenician child sacrifice in: Paolo Xella, Josephine Quinn, Valentina Melchiorri and Peter van Dommelen. "Phoenician Bones of Contention." *Antiquity* 87 (2013) 1199-1207; also see the volume: Paolo Xella, ed. *The Tophet in the Phoenician Mediterranean.* Studi Epigrafi Linguistici 30 (2012); also B. Doak et al., *Oxford Handbook of the Phoenician and Punic Mediterranean.* Oxford: Oxford University Press, 2019.

8   David Soren, Aicha Ben Abed Ben Khader, Hedi Slim, *Carthage; Uncovering the Mysteries and Splendors of Ancient Tunisia.* New York: Simon and Schuster, 1990, 236.

9   Kaufmann Kohler and Ludwig Blau, "Gehenna," in the *Jewish Encyclopedia* (1906 edition). (http://www.jewishencyclopedia.com/articles/6558-gehenna).

10   Lloyd R. Bailley, "The Topography of Hell," *Biblical Archeologist* (1986), 187-91, esp. 189.

11   Yuval Gadot, "Jerusalem and the Holy Land[fill]," *Biblical Archaeology Review*, Jan/Feb 2018; Megan Sauter. "Taking Out the Trash in Ancient Jerusalem." *Bible History Daily (Online).* January 9, 2018. BAS (Biblical Archaeology Society). Although some debate a trash dump, instead thinking Roman destruction around 70 CE, most of it being organic matter make a garbage dump most likely. (https://www.biblicalarchaeology.org/daily/ancient-cultures/daily-life-and-practice/garbage-archaeology-ancient-jerusalem/).

7

Translating *Alabastron* in Mark 14:3: an Archaeological Solution to a Philological Problem?

❖

End of Mark's Gospel, Codex Vaticanus, Early 4th c., mostly ch. 16

"While he was in Bethany, reclining at the table in the home of Simon the Leper, a woman came with an alabaster jar of very expensive perfume, made of pure nard. She broke the jar and poured the perfume on his head." Mark 14:3 (NIV)

Many questions arise from this familiar text even in comparison with the other synoptic gospel texts of the same story. Although not often asked, one of the most enigmatic is why the vessel was broken? Alabaster as the stone medium here may raise more questions than answers even though this is the traditional translation of *alabastron* ("alabaster jar" in the NIV above). Some of the questions include the following: Which was more valuable, the alabaster vessel or the perfume? If the vessel was sealed to preserve the nard, why would it have to be broken to access the perfume? Was this a waste of a good alabaster vessel regardless of the valuable perfume inside? Perhaps most important, what if the perfume vessel wasn't now actually alabaster stone, but instead, but instead, it retained its common name *alabastron,* from its earlier alabaster form?

Thus this set of problematic synoptic texts deserves attention. The familiar gospel story (Mark 14:3; also Luke 7:37-8, Matthew 26:7 as well as John 12:3) is also voluminously depicted in art:[1] a woman breaks a vessel of perfume (ἀλάβαστρον) and washes Jesus's head or feet with the expensive perfume. Caravaggio is one of the very few artists who renders a translucent glass vessel rather than alabaster stone, not the least to showcase his virtuosity in showing light through liquid. Nearly all translations render the word ἀλάβαστρον for the vessel as being of alabaster. But how likely is this? A little archaeological and philological history might offer better possibilities.

As suggested, what if the value of this offering is not so much in the precious stone alabaster but the actual perfume (νάρδος, *nardos* in Greek), "pure nard" from the exotic spikenard plant *Nardostachys jatamansi* ssp.) possibly imported all the way from Himalayan India and which many perfumes aimed to imitate?[2] This emphasis is implied in expanded versions of the story in Matthew 26:12-13, where Jesus says the expensive value is appropriate because it was done as a memorial: "In pouring this ointment on my body, she has done it to prepare me for burial. Truly, I say to you, wherever this gospel is proclaimed in the whole world, what she has done will also be told in memory of her." Jesus doesn't at all note or lament the vessel breakage—never he does suggest that breaking an expensive vessel was memorable—but he emphatically justifies this expensive ointment use as proleptic of his impending death. The extremely high value of the expensive nard is often estimated as around 300 denarii, almost a year's wage for a typical work at this time, hence the objection of some of those present in the following verses (Mark 14:4-5) who deemed it a waste.[3]

The text states that the woman had an "*alabastron* of pure nard ointment" (ἀλάβαστρον μύρου νάρδου πιστικῆς) where *pistikes* is "pure."[4] The value of spikenard was enormous, consumed by the wealthy but appreciated by poets: in the

Nardostachys jatamansi—
Himalayan plant source of spikenard

late first c. BCE the Roman poet Horace promised his famous poet friend Virgil, author of the *Aeneid,* a whole *cadus* (~36 quarts) of wine in exchange for a small onyx box of spikenard in his poem *Carmen* 4. xii. lines 16-17.

If we examine the word *alabastron* (ἀλάβαστρον), normally translated "phial, bottle or vessel", from both philological and archaeological perspectives, historical facts emerge. Here in Mark 14:3 it is a direct object, hence the ending in ν ("*n*") but it would have the same ending if either nominative or accusative when neuter, but when it is masculine (*alabastros* in nominative, subject case), it would only end in ν ("*n*") if it were in the accusative case as direct object.

Archaeologically, an *alabastron* is a very common name for a perfume vessel regardless of its medium (normally stone, ceramic, glass) especially from Classical, Ptolemaic and Hellenistic cultures.[5] Faience is another, less common medium for an alabastron.[6] There are too many ceramic *alabastra* to count, most often in red or black figure style, but even in white-slipped ceramic that resembles alabaster, possibly intentionally. Glass *alabastra* are certainly common in Italy, Greece, and the Levant in

Alabaster stone alabastron, Cypriot, 5th-4th c, BCE Metropolitan Museum, New York, Cesnola Collection, Acc. # 74.51.5093

the Hellenistic period (late 4th to 1st c. BCE). Based on extant museum examples, the distribution likelihood of the preferred medium for *alabastra* suggest that the higher quantities were ceramic and glass, not alabaster, in the Roman period.

Most lexical discussions of the noun *alabastron* note that it originated as likely alabaster stone (banded calcite), especially from the initial point of contact with Egypt where alabaster was common as an unguent vessel, not only from the Bronze Age onwards but especially around the Greek trading colony of Naukratis in Egypt 7th c. BCE onward on the Canopic Nile, as

White-Ground Ceramic "Paisadic" Attic painted alabastron, ca 520-500 BCE British Museum (#1887,0801.61)

the Greek historian traveler Herodotus relates in his *History* 2.178-9, as the original *alabastra* vessels—mostly cylindrical in shape—were made of alabaster. Note several Naukratis alabaster stone *alabastra* in Penn Museum, Ashmolean Museum and Boston Museum of Fine Art, from 7th c. BCE to 4th c. [6a-b-c] or from Late Dynastic XXVI/XXVII to Ptolemaic Periods. The production of Egyptian alabaster stone alabaster at Naukratis continues into the Roman Era: "alabaster vessels…still produced in the Roman Period."[7] Even Pliny observes that unguents "keep best in alabaster," but this is somewhat ambiguous in translation, since he uses the word *alabastris* (dative for indirect object) instead of a form of *alabastrites*.[8,9]

Glass perfume alabastron, 2nd-1st c. BCE, Louvre Museum, Dept. of Greek, Roman, Etruscan Antiquities, 3.5 in h, Acc. # S2375, acquired from Italy, Campana Collection, 1861

Both ceramic and glass soon rival alabaster stone as media for perfume vessels in Egypt and elsewhere from the Hellenistic and Roman world. I have seen countless more extant ceramic and glass *alabastra* rather than the rarer and older alabaster (mostly from earlier Egypt as already noted). Above is an Egyptian-style glass *alabastron* from Magna Graecia (Southern Italy) of the 2nd-1st c. BCE in the Louvre Collection.

Opaque white glass—possibly imitating alabaster stone—could be achieved by adding alumina to the glass melt, as also seen below in a Christie's 1st c. CE white glass *alabastron*.

So many other glass *alabastron* examples from the Hellenistic and Roman periods can be found with even minimal effort in many museums, as seen below from the National Archaeology Museum of Florence or from the Corning Museum of Glass, which also has a glass *alabastron* from the 2nd to 1st c. Eastern Mediterranean (Acc. #66.1.229).

Equally, the Archaeological Museum of Tarquinia has Hellenistic glass *alabastra* in display, seen below as item 24 in the case vitrine, since the Hellenized Etruscans had either perfected the technology or imported the craft from the East via Phoenician traders or Greeks in Southern Italy influenced by Ptolemaic Egypt. Ennion was a 1st c. CE famous glassmaker from Sidon in the Roman province of Syria, where a large bulk of Roman glass was produced.[10] Roman glassblowing emerged in the first half of the 1st c. CE in central Italy after Etrurian and Southern Italian ventures.[11]

Christie's London July 6 2016 Catalog: "Roman Opaque white glass alabastron, circa 1st c. AD"

Glass could be had very cheap by the Roman Era, as Strabo notes in *Geography* XVI.2 that a single copper coin could purchase a glass cup, although some artistic glass was also valuable. It is most likely, however, that the perfume was far more valuable than the vessel.

Returning to the definitions of *alabastron*, *The Greek-English Lexicon* (Liddell & Scott) states an *alabastron* may be made of alabaster but is not limited to this medium.[12] *Strong's Concordance* also notes that the *alabastron* is not *exclusively* crafted from alabaster stone.[13] Thus, along with the Oxford Classical Art Research Center-Beazley Archive definition (already stated in note 4 above), it was made in a "range of materials." So how did all the translations limit the meanings to only alabaster stone? One possibility is the prevalence of tradition. It may well be that when Jerome (late 4th c. CE) translated the Greek New

Museum of Tarquinia, Italy, Hellenistic glass alabastra, (P. Hunt photo, 2013)

Testament into the Latin Vulgate in a period of huge literacy decline, he rendered the Greek *alabastron* into the Latin *alabastrum*, making it more likely to be translated as alabaster stone in a tradition that has lasted for more than two and a half millennia.

Now the speculative part: was the New Testament vessel "broken" (συντρίψασα) because the completely-sealed top of it was otherwise intended to preserve it so well that it had to be broken? In the 5th c. Augustine states the whole vessel was broken but Barnes suggests it was only the seal that was broken[14] perhaps to get around the problem of "breaking" a whole vessel, especially alabaster stone precious in its own right. But given the possibly long distance travel involved, a fused glass *alabastron* ampule would far better preserve the perfume, especially for a one-off use.

Fusing glass is not hard, as Roman and Levant craftspersons had mastered adding stoppers as well as handles and decorative pieces. Silica normally melts at around 1400° C but is malleable at "glass transformation temperature" (GTT) much lower around 580° C for soda-lime-silica. Temperatures around 1000° C were easily achievable in metallurgy in antiquity (since the melting point of both gold and copper required melting the silicate rock ore) and in ancient glass manufacturing, salt or lead were commonly added as a flux to further lower the temperature significantly. But glass was soft and bondable in a much lower and wider temperature range as can be seen from the above GTT at around 580° C. The longer the neck of a glass *alabastron*, the easier to twist, pinch or otherwise seal the vessel without affecting the nard inside, although some heat could even improve the unguent provided it wouldn't volatilize or vaporize outside the vessel. Certainly sealing the glass with sufficient heat would best preserve the perfume. Clear glass would not be so efficient because light could break down (photolysis) the perfume even if the perfume was a compressed sap of nard embedded or floating in olive oil or other unguent, but if the perfume had nowhere to evacuate because the seal was permanent this would be less a problem. Dried out nard would be much less valuable, so sealing it was vital, especially if transported over distance.

Again, back to the question of breaking the vessel, why would one have to "break" (συντρίψασα in the Koine Greek of Mark 14:3 and variants of it elsewhere) the perfume vessel if it were carved alabaster, which could never be completely sealed anyway as well as glass, which could be completely sealed by heat without destroying the nard inside, especially if in a long-necked glass *alabastron*? The logical options are that breaking the vessel was either extravagant or necessary. Another hermeneutic possibility must be considered: was the *alabastron* broken because it was a symbolic act, a one-off that meant the vessel would be profaned if used again? Plus was it also symbolic of Jesus being "broken" in sacrificial death?

In conclusion, the meaning of the word 'alabastron must be reconsidered in translations that render it as stone. Although the original meaning in the Greek Archaic and Classical periods ca. 600-400 BCE as seen in Egypt in the Greek colony at Naukratis would have been alabaster stone, by the Hellenistic world ca. 300 BCE, this material was changing to ceramic and eventually more likely to glass in higher frequency by the Roman period ca. 100 BCE to 100 CE. while still retaining the original name, as the vessels depicted here show. Certainly more questions arise, but it is no longer a given that the vessel described in the New Testament gospels had to be alabaster stone, which trammels the value of the more precious spikenard itself.

❖

Endnotes Chapter 7

1   Patrick Hunt, "Irony and Realism in the Iconography of Caravaggio's penitent Magdalene," chapter 6, in M. A. Erhardt and A. M. Morris, eds., *Mary Magdalene, Iconographic Studies from the Middle Ages to the Baroque.* Studies in Religion and the Arts, vol. 7. Leiden: E. J. Brill, 2012, 161-86, esp. 175-77.

2   Pliny, *Natural History* XIII.2 also states that the viscous "unguent of cinnamon… has an enormous price…up to 300 denarii per pound" and many perfumes aim to "imitate Indian nard" (*Nardostachys jatamansi* ssp.).

3   There is some debate whether *pistikes* means pure but the majority consensus suggests this.

4   Oxford Classical Art Research Center—Beasley Archive, under "*alabastron*": "a long-bodied vessel…long history in Corinth… Examples have been found in a range of materials, including alabaster. The Greek term for this stone—'**alabastron** (probably of Egyptian origin—probably reveals the inspiration for the shape, and many [ceramic] examples are covered with white-ground, as it to imitate the stone. It seems primarily to have been a vessel for perfumed oil…" (https://www.beazley.ox.ac.uk/tools/pottery/shapes/alabastron.htm).

5   While faience appears to be a rare medium for perfume *alabastra,* some can be found from, for example, 7th c. BCE Etruscan Cerveteri (Tomb 111, Monte Abatone) as well as the Fusco Necropolis (Tomb 85) of Siracusa (Sicily) and Phoenician Motya (Sicily), another one claiming to be faience is at the Getty Villa in Los Angeles (#88.AI.135), among others; whether they were all manufactured in Rhodes or elsewhere may be arguable but they were known to be exported to the rest of the Mediterranean. See Federica Galiffa, "A new faïance alabastron with figurative decoration from Cerveteri,"*Abstracts of the Crafts of the European Iron Age Conference*, Cambridge, September 2015, 25 (http://www.arch.cam.ac.uk/iron_age/craft).

6   Penn Museum # AN1120293001001, E47, published by A. Villing et al., *Naukratis: Greeks in Egypt*. London: British Museum, 2013-15 (#EA 001). [6b] Ashmolean Museum, Oxford #AN1407611001001 (#AN1896-1908-E.3695), also published by A. Villing et al., *Naukratis: Greeks in Egypt*. London: British Museum, 2013-15 (#EA 004). [6c] Also note the Naukratis alabaster stone *alabastron* at the Boston Museum of Fine Art #AN1275621001001 (Accession no. # RES 88-40), again published by A. Villing et al., *Naukratis: Greeks in Egypt*. London: British Museum, 2013-15 (#EA 007).

7   B. G. Aston, *Ancient Egyptian stone vessels: materials and forms*. Heidelberger Orientverlag, Heidelberg, 1994; A. Masson, 'Le quartier des prêtres du temple de Karnak: rapport préliminaire de la fouille de la maison VII, 2001-2003,' *Cahiers de Karnak* XII, 2007, 593-655, esp. 612, plate XXVIII no. 1-3. [British Museum curator comments: http://www.britishmuseum.org/research/publications/online_research_catalogues/search_object_details.aspx].

8   Pliny, *Natural History* XIII.3: *unguenta optime servantur in alabastris*: which is ambiguous because it is unclear whether *alabastris* are vessels made of alabaster or merely the vessel form known as *alabastra*.

9   *Alabastrites* is clearly a Latin word for alabaster stone "stone composed of carbonate of lime…precious stone found in Egypt" *Harpers Latin Dictionary* (Andrews-Freund, revised Lewis and Short), 1907, 79.

10   Christopher Lightfoot et al., *Ennion: Master of Roman Glass*. Metropolitan Museum of Art, New York, 2015.

11   Rosemary Trentinella, "Roman Glass," Metropolitan Museum of Art, *Heilbrunn Timeline of Art History*, 2003.

12   H. G. Liddell and R. Scott, eds. "often" made of alabaster [but not limited to this medium] in earlier citations than in the New Testament, *Greek-English Lexicon*, Oxford: Clarendon Press, 1996 ed., 59.

13   James Strong, *Exhaustive Concordance*. Entry # 211 "alabastron."

14 Interestingly, in Augustine *De consensu evangeliorum* (Harmony of the Gospels 278) LXXIX.155, Augustine states the whole vessel was broken. Albert Barnes, *Notes on the Old and New Testaments*, vol. 9. *The Gospels*, Baker Books, (originally 1870) 1983, 381 (Mark:14:3).

8

Corinthian Bronze, Demeter, and *Glossalalia* in I Corinthians 8, 13, 14

❖

Corinthian-style Bronze Helmet, 5th c. Houston Museum of Art (P. Hunt)

Corinth is one of the oldest, richest cities of the Greek world, described by Strabo as "wealthy Corinth" for its location and commerce.[1] That is no wonder, given its highly strategic location on the Isthmus of Corinth linking it by land to Attica and Boeotia north on mainland Greece and to the Peloponnesus south since the Bronze Age. Equally important, Corinth also connected the Aegean to the Gulf of Corinth by sea and guaranteed far safer passage than by sailing south around the dangerous Cape Malea at the southern rugged tip of the Aegean. Corinth thus had ports on both sides at Lechaion on the west of the isthmus and Cenchreae on the east of the isthmus.[2] Writers and poets like Propertius and proverbs warned ships against passing by Malea: "Round Cape Malea and forget about home…" as strong winds in winter easily exceed 30 miles per hour on a normal basis and even in summer in sailing season at least a quarter of the time.[3] The shipping taxes and surcharges Corinth acquired from this dual maritime and unique land location contributed greatly to its prosperity.

The name of the city is also one of the oldest in the Greek world and is likely Pre-Greek in the sense of Late Bronze Age Mycenaean morphemes, possibly named after the mountain looming overhead.[4] I have also speculated "Corinth" could mean "Place (-inth) of the Maiden (Kore)", but whether this could reference the goddesses Persephone or Aphrodite is ambiguous, since it could also be from either source (or not at all) given the world-famous Temple of Aphrodite on the Acrocorinth above the city—itself 6th-5th c. BCE although the Aphrodite cult there is older—or the ancient sanctuary of Demeter and Persephone whose sacred precincts surround the region of Corinth since at least the 11th c. BCE.[5] Legend states that Kypselos was the 7th c. tyrant of Corinth in whose Archaic Era the Aphrodite cult had a likely hyperbolic number of 1,000 temple courtesans (hetairai or hierodouloi) of both sexes according to Strabo[6], whereas in a much-debated text Pindar partly verifies the courtesans and practices although not the quantity.[7] Strongly associating Corinth with Aphrodite, there may be ample ancient texts suggesting Corinth was at times even called the "City of Aphrodite," either as an epithet or merely as a description.[8] While having so many legendary courtesans in the Roman Era is highly unlikely, there was still enough activity for its temple prostitution to be famous. It seems logical that Corinth would be understandably associated with problematic porneia as in Paul's discourse in I Corinthians 6:12-20, however difficult to translate and one of the most debated topics in the biblical literature.[9] That the believers in the formative Corinthian church—according to I Cornithians 3:1 and the following discourse—were partly evaluated as "carnal" or "fleshly" (σαρχίνοις in Greek) may be related to the overall atmosphere of Corinth as an Aphrodite center that even permeated or impacted the new Christian community.

Given there is near consensus among scholars across the spectrum that Paul was in Corinth for several years circa 49-51 CE, many commentators have examined both Pauline epistolary texts of I, II Corinthians, among others, and the Acts of the Apostles in light of voluminous archaeological evidence from Corinth contexts, especially in the more than a century since 1896 that the American School of Classical Studies, Athens, has extensively excavated and documented Corinth, including Roman Corinth, in many scholarly volumes. Because Ancient Corinth was not underneath modern Corinth, the latter having mostly moved away from the site, the archaeological investigations can yield enormous detail for antiquity. Three of the topics that can be newly examined here relative to Paul's writing to the Corinthians include Corinthian bronze history, the Demeter and Persephone sanctuary ritual food and the practice of *glossalalia* ("tongues") at Corinth, among other subjects. Others have written much about the Corinth theater "Erastus Pavement" and the nearby Isthmian games that Paul seems to have attended given his multiple references to sporting events, so these will not be mentioned except in passing, since the primary emphases in this chapter will be on the several topics highlighted above with new insights in I Corinthians 8, 13, 14, (though not necessarily in that order).

Because mercantilism and skilled craft production, along with wide distribution of luxury goods, were vital to its business successes, Corinth was also one of the Greek leaders in Mediterranean trade, transport and colonizing. The city had established early to mid 1st millennium BCE trading with the Egyptian Delta at Naukratis (note Corinthian pottery is the earliest Greek pottery at Naukratis[10]) and in the Levant at Ras Mina (where it is again represented very early and also very early at Pithecusae in Italy[11]) as well as its own colony in Sicily at Siracusa and other Ionian Sea sites. Corinthian pottery, distinctive for its Orientalizing motif of borrowed Near Eastern and Egyptian myth motif and creamy color, can be found throughout the Mediterranean world, especially Corinthian decorated perfume and cosmetic vessels (*aryballos, pyxis, alabastron*, etc.), and

Corinthian wine amphorae are also widespread across the Mediterranean in the Archaic period from 8th c. BCE onward.[12] Easily one of Corinth's most respected crafts—perhaps the most famous—was bronze working. There are different types of bronze production in Corinth, including in the materials and techniques. Whether in distinctive Corinthian-style helmet production—often hammered out from a single bronze sheet—or making weapons and even medical tools, Corinth was justly famous for bronze.[13] There were known workshops for bronze production in Corinth of a range of various products.[14]

But there was also a special status for what was called "Corinthian Bronze"—(χαλκός Κόρινθου, *chalkos Korinthou*) also known as *aes Corinthiacum* in Latin—in antiquity as the most prized bronze in the Classical world, especially when gold and silver were in the alloy with copper, as Pliny and others relate, although it is not necessarily easy to pin down its exact composition.[15] Pliny may describe at least three alloy based colors of Corinthian bronze depending on the alloy percentage of copper, gold and silver; others note even a purple hue of "Corinthian Bronze" for the most valuable medical tools made of various bronzes of Corinth and some also note the possibility of "dyeing" bronze for different hues based on alloys.[16] This prized bronze had separate applications from usual bronze use for tools and armor because "Corinthian Bronze" would likely be softer and hence less practical for normal use as well as beautiful to look at,[17] even when other bronzes likely corroded or patinated more easily, as Cicero and Plutarch asserted. Gold does not easily corrode and even silver is relatively stable, tarnishing slowly relative to normal copper oxidation with its range of green patination.[18] Sometimes the term "Corinthian Bronze" refers more to this alloy itself than to Corinthian production of the prized alloy and it could have been made anywhere such as Egypt using depletion gilding and other alloy processes.[19] Nonetheless Corinth was justifiably famous for valued bronze and its citizens proud of it. Even the Temple in Jerusalem had its great Nicanor Gate doors embellished with world-famous and precious "Corinthian Bronze" from Herod's lavish rebuilding in the late 1st c. BCE, as Josephus notes[20] and of which costly furnishing Paul likely was aware.

Musical instruments were also crafted in sought-after bronze from Corinth, an alloy also likely known for its acoustic quality, including sets of cymbals and the sistrum, although not necessarily made from the prized and precious metal alloy Pliny and others knew as "Corinthian Bronze" but merely bronze from Corinth. A bronze 1st c. CE sistrum at the Metropolitan Museum, New York, is an example of a musical instrument, although its provenance is unknown, possibly Egypt or South Italy or elsewhere.[21] A set of Greek bronze cymbals also at the Metropolitan Museum, ca. 5th-4th c. BCE, and attributed to the Peloponnesus is another example, more likely from Corinth.[22] Both musical instruments were most likely used in religious contexts for ecstatic or ritual celebration, especially the cymbals used in "Demeter, Dionysus and Cybele worship,"[23] and the sistrum often had associations with Egyptian Isis cultic contexts, as can be seen in Roman wall paintings from Herculaneum and Pompeii depicting Isis Temple scenes, both seen in the Archaeological Museum of Naples, where priests or participants hold the sistrum.[24] There were definitely Egyptian Isis cult contexts in and around Corinth where such musical instruments would have been used ritually, including at Cenchreae near the port (*'Isidos hiera*).[25] Apuleius later (2nd c. CE) describes activities here because Isis centers ritually opened up the sea at springtime (*Navigium Isidis*), even in his fictionalized account of Lucius and his transformation.[26]

Many have considered whether Paul is alluding to Corinth's historic rich bronze traditions in I Corinthians 13: 1: "If I speak in the tongues of men and angels and have not love, I become as sounding bronze or ringing cymbals."

Some of these commentators include Harris, Klein, O'Connor, Witherington and others,[27] and while O'Connor correctly surmises "Corinthian

Peloponnesian Bronze Cymbal 5th-4th c. BCE, Metropolitan Museum of Art, New York (courtesy Metropolitan Museum of Art)

Bronze" isn't the only famous bronze product of Corinth, Witherington maintains *chalkos* is never used in any ancient text for a musical instrument. While it may well be that *chalkos* by itself is not mentioned, in earlier Greek, Pindar's *Isthmian Ode* 7.6.3, the music accompanying Demeter celebrations indeed uses the Greek word *chalkokrotos,* which can be translated "sounding or rattling with bronze" as an "epithet of Demeter, in allusion to instruments used in her worship."[28] One translation of this passage in Pindar's *Isthmian Ode* 7 literally reads *chalkokrotou* (gen. s.) in the line "seated beside Demeter *of the clashing bronze cymbals* [italics added]."[29] Although Pindar's line references Demeter as well as Dionysus, Race notes about these lines "…it was Kybele who was normally associated with clanging of cymbals,"[30] a Kybele connection repeated through other ancient Greek musicology studies of Euripides' *Helen* 1358-52 and the *Deipnosophistae* 621b-d. At times bronze cymbals are connected with Aphrodite in literature,[31] both of which deities are known in Roman Corinth. In any case, the Pindaric lines closely resemble Paul's metaphor.

Additionally, though obscure, other Greek compounds or derivatives of *chalkos* that are related to sound can be found, for example, in *phone chalkizousa,* "ring like brass" in Pollux Grammaticus, *Onomasticon* (2.117) as well as his *chalkophonos* "sound like bronze" (2.111)[32] although these are clearly later than Paul in the 2nd-3rd c. CE and possibly even linked to this passage in I Corinthians 13:1. But earlier in 4th-3rd c. BCE there is in a Menander fragment ([Libanius] *Declamation* 26.1.34) and repeated in a Late Greek proverb of Stephanos of Byzantium, an expression *Dodonaion chalkeion* (or *chalkion*) "the Dodona bronze vessel," which can be read as "babbler or chatterbox" where *chalkeion* can also be a metaphoric gloss for a "cymbal," possibly significant or hypothetically even having influenced Paul because of excess in speaking and possibly an allusion to oracular tongues, to be developed further.[33]

As for the acoustic word *krotos* alone, in addition to its above compound with *chalkokrotos,* it has several musical connotations. One is found in dance with the "beat of feet" and the other in the "striking" of lyre strings (*kroteta pektidon mele*) derived from the verb *kroteo* in the 3rd c. BCE.[34]

Thus, there is clearly sufficient archaeological (material) and textual (literary) history bound up in aspects of bronze in local Corinthian contexts for Paul to be alluding in I Corinthians 13:1 to known dual traditions his audience could recognize in both civic pride in famous Corinth's bronze tradecraft and in contemporary religious connotations of musical associations of bronze musical instruments with either Demeter or Isis, since both had important centers in or around Corinth, especially the Demeter connections to be enlarged next in I Corinthians 8:1.

This brings us to the next passage, I Corinthians 8:1: "Now concerning things sacrificed to idols" (εἰδωλοθύτων is "sacrificed to idols"), where the obvious context is confirmed in 8:4 and repeated in 8:7 as "to eat thing[s] sacrificed to an idol" (εἰδωλόθυτον ἐσθίουσιν is "eat [ἐσθίουσιν] a thing sacrificed to an idol" [εἰδωλόθυτον]). This discourse could apply to many possible Greek cultic offerings in Corinth. But the likelihood of the highest probable source, unless split among many, points to the Demeter and Persephone cult center at Corinth, the largest, just above the Roman and former Greek city rather than to the Aphrodite cult high above on the Acrocorinth and the more distant.

We already know the most common animal sacrificed to Demeter and Persephone was a pig, often a young one,[35] even modeled in clay votives offered at Corinth, both singly and carried by female offerants.[36] But in what may be a fairly remarkable correlation between I Corinthians 8:1-4 and the archaeological record at Corinth, American School of Classical Studies at Athens (ASCSA) Corinth excavator Dr. Nancy Bookidis shared with me personally in 1984 when I was a graduate student there that after 146 BCE when the Romans under Mummius sacked Corinth, the usual Demeter and Kore sanctuary practices changed. The sanctuary then had a hiatus for a century. Excavations at the sanctuary showed generations of prior feasting of pigs onsite prior to the mid-2nd c. BCE, with the fauna of pig-only bones buried in pits within the sanctuary.[37] But the inference of what changed is that when the Roman city was re-established, the votive offerings of pigs continued as normal at the sanctuary—too high frequency a Demeter and Kore tradition even into the Roman Era[38]—but there were no more communal feasts and hence no burial pig bone pits after 146 BCE; with the likelihood that the meat was instead sold at the Corinth Agora. This makes sense in interpreting this Corinthian text with specific detail, although any such meat sold from offered animals in the context of Paul's reference could also be from cultic sacrifices to other deities, and not only pig. On the other hand, Newton claims (p. 59) there is insufficient evidence for the connection of I Corinthians 8:1 to be made to the Demeter and Kore sanctuary at Corinth. Nonetheless, the fact that the Demeter and Kore sanctuary provides a direct correlation for contextualizing this I Corinthians 8:1-4 reference makes the connection highly plausible.

The last passage to be examined here is I Corinthians 14 on what is termed *glossalalia*—a word primarily only found in modern interpretation—or translated as the "ecstatic practice of speaking in tongues." The term is extrapolated from the original Greek *glossa* (γλῶσσα) for 1) "tongue" and 2) "language" in the Ionic (and Doric) dialect of the Peloponnesus where Corinth is located.[39] This is a contentious matter not only to secular scholars but equally so to the Christian community, and church history is divided on what "tongues" and "speaking in tongues" mean as an apostolic spiritual gift as outlined in the New Testament[40] and where a majority consensus is difficult to reach whether the spiritual gift ceased with the end of the Apostolic Age or continues beyond. Equally problematic is the conundrum of tongues in Corinth where tongues was apparently often a divisive and hierarchical issue in the local church there. How to define what "tongues," "speaking in tongues" or the Greek derivative *glossalalia* comprised remains enigmatic in part due to the linguistic discontinuity between the ancient and modern worlds. Some have even argued, from Carlyle May and Dunn onward, that what was manifest at Corinth may have been more of a broader Hellenistic phenomenon and not a uniquely Christian spiritual gift.[41] How to separate the possible phenomena of Classical mantic utterance from Christian *glossalalia*—if different—is not easily apparent, especially since the Greek word *glossalalia* may not be itself ancient.

Delphic Oracle Kylix, Kodros Painter
ca. 440-430 BCE, Berlin Anitkensammlung
Berlin, Altes Museum (Photo P. Hunt)

Ancient history shows at least by the 5th c. BCE both Herodotus and Aeschylus identified ecstatic and mantic prophecy in highly idiosyncratic speech utterances difficult to interpret. Diodorus Siculus also describes the oracular gifts of Daphne, daughter of the prophet Tiresias, who had gifts to speak "inspired by her tongue...for to be inspired on one's tongue is expressed by the word *sibyllainein*"[42] Naturally, Dunn and Forbes above have examined the parallels of Christian *glossalalia* with the Delphic Oracle, the latter involving a mantic priestess whose utterances must be interpreted by the Delphic Hierophant in often equally enigmatic results. Others like Forbes also remind from Classical literature the comparable mantic tradition Virgil retells in *Aeneid* 6 of the Sibyl of Cumae who, when filled with the spirit of Apollo prophesies the future of Aeneas in almost unintelligible utterances that must be interpreted.[43]

But too often unknown or ignored is the fact that Corinth is surrounded by oracles whose interpretive practices are closer to Corinthian *glossalalia* and Delphic utterances, all of which must be interpreted, not only at Delphi with Apollo's Pythia and ecstatic speech,[44] but also Cybele cultic trances at Corinth[45] and the Oracle of Trophonios at Livadia. Other Greek oracles include much further to the north in the Epirus at Dodona, an oracle perhaps second only to Delphi and rich in Classical citations including Plato's *Phaedra* 244b, Cicero' *De Divinatione* Diodorus Siculus' *Bib. Hist.* 18.4.4, Plutarch's *Lysander* 25.3 and Pausanias' *Travels* 8.23.5.[46] Interesting perhaps is that Plato questions whether the Dodona priestesses might have at times been "mad"—whatever that means—and discusses their being "in their right minds" as opposed to not being so. Both Trophonios and Dodona are similar to Corinthian tongues because the utterances of nature must be interpreted by priestly intermediaries. At Livadia, the Trophonios Oracle was a water-based fountain oracle with a Cave of Dreams and where one drank of different streams—Memory and Forgetfulness—with often dangerous effects. Another form of the Trophonios Oracle was direct contact via water, however, where Trophonios had an acoustic oracle derived from the burbling of the stream eroding under the river and which needed someone to interpret the water noises.[47] At Dodona, the wind moving through the leaves of the great Dodona oak tree also makes rustling leaf utterances the priests must interpret. Additionally, the mantic *glossalalia* of the prophetess Cassandra is literarily represented from Pillinger's new study of Classical *glossalalia*.[48] Other oracles of the Peloponnesus not far from Corinth include the famous Oracle of Zeus at Olympia[49] and the Oracle of Bakis of Arcadia to the south.[50] Clearly, the word "oracle" itself in antiquity implies an oral medium of communication of quasi-supernatural or prophetic information that must be officially interpreted by religious authority.

The familiarity of Corinth with ecstatic speech of mantic prophets is assumed by its Peloponnese proximity to some of these Greek oracles such as Trophonios, Delphi, Olympia, Bakis and other Arcadian shrines—at least four regional oracles—where oracles appear to have thrived in the ancient world. Did these local oracles influence the behavior of Corinth in any way to emphasize the mantic *glossalalia* there, or was the spiritual gift of "tongues" there unique to Christianity? Clearly by referencing angelic language, Paul alludes to possible supernatural sources Greeks would accept. We may never know but the question will likely remain contentious.

Two other brief discussions relative to Corinth and the Pauline epistles that have received considerable attention are the likely references to the nearby Isthmian Games Paul appears to have attended around 49-50 CE and the Erastus Pavement adjoining the Corinthian Theater. First, I Corinthians 9:24-27 offers multiple examples of athletic events Paul would have viewed:

Do you not know that in a race all the runners run, but only one gets the prize? Run in such a way as to get the prize. Everyone who competes in the games goes into strict training. They do it to get a crown that will not last, but we do it to get a crown that will last forever. Therefore I do not run like someone running aimlessly; I do not fight like a boxer beating the air. No, I strike a blow to my body and make it my slave so that after I have preached to others, I myself will not be disqualified for the prize.

Here with figurative language Paul offers insights into spiritual discipline that parallels physical discipline. As found in Swaddling's surveys of Greek Panhellenic Games (*'agonai*),[51] he first mentions running on the Isthmian *stade* course that would include the 200-meter sprint and the longer *dolichos* course, with both events often shown in Greek vases even into the Roman Era. He continues with allusions to the vegetal crowns and wreaths offered to victors; at Isthmia it was a celery wreath, which clearly would wilt rather quickly. These vegetal crowns (along with olive at Olympia and Nemea, as well as laurel at Delphi) emphasize, just as Paul confirms, that they are ephemeral rewards offered by human hands. This is partly because the Greeks understood each game result to be temporary with new winners regularly, so ephemerality was part of the philosophic intent. Also prominent in the figurative athletic language of the above text is boxing, again part of Isthmia's long traditions, whether with bare hands or gloves and hand wraps as depicted in many Greek vases and sculptures. Broneer was one of the first to publish these likely athletic references to Isthmia.[52] Such depiction of both foot races ands boxing can be readily seen in the British Museum public collections. Other Pauline texts that reference the type of games Paul would have witnessed if an attendee include I Timothy 2:5 & 6:12 as well as II Timothy 4:7. Although not considered as Pauline authorship—but possibly by Apollos who was likewise attested at Corinth in Acts of the Apostles and the Corinthian epistles, Hebrews 12:1-2 also references foot races.[53] These athletic references appear to confirm their authors being spectators at the repeated Greek *'agonai* of Isthmia.

The final brief discussion on the famous Erastus Pavement adjacent to the theater at Corinth has little new to add. Kent first published this in 1936 for the American School of Classical Studies of Athens excavations at Corinth and most commentators argue for this pavement naming the same person as Romans 16:23. The Latin inscription of the Erastus Pavement reads ERASTUS PRO AEDILIT[AT]E S[UA] P[ECUNIA] STRAVIT: "Erastus in return for his aedileship paved this with his own money." Excavated in 1929, Kent stated "the original suggestion that Erastus is to be identified with the Corinthian Erastus of the NT (Romans 16:23) still seems sound" and this American School of Classical Studies at Athens declaration has not been soundly argued against since.[54] When I was in Corinth, as mentioned earlier, as a graduate student in 1984 at the American School of Classical Studies (ASCSA), it was Dr. Charles Williams, the ASCSA Corinth Excavations Director (1966-97), who personally took me to examine the Erastus Pavement and discuss it with me relative to Paul's time in Corinth. His opinion was consonant with Kent and the consensus of subsequent commentators who find it credibly connected to the same Erasmus of Romans 16:23. The Greek word (οἰκονόμος, 'oikonómos) in the Romans passage as "City Steward" or "Director of Public Works" is sufficiently close in function to the Latin *aedile,* as Kent states, "with reasonable accuracy."[55] The *aedile* or 'oikonómos would have been a wealthy private citizen holding office, able and expected to pay for such work projects at his own expense, exactly as the inscription reads. This is a direct

ERASTUS Pavement, Corinth, ca. 49 CE *(Photo P. Hunt)*

synchronicity between a Corinthian inscription and a New Testament text, contextualizing and corroborating the biblical account.

Last but not least, other possible Demeter and Persephone (Kore) connections in I Corinthians include the multiple references to "mysteries" (e.g., 13:2, 14:2, 15:51) and the references to "first fruit" (ἀπαρχὴ, *aparche*) including in I Corinthians 15:20 & 23. The Eleusinian Mysteries of Demeter and Persephone were the most Greek of all and held at Eleusis in Attica near Athens but also had satellite centers at places like the sanctuary at Corinth.[56] The word "mysteries" (μυστήρια in Greek) refers to something private for the initiates of mysteries like the Eleusinian, since *mystes* (μύστης in Greek) is "initiate." Paul could have possibly learned much about the Eleusinian Mysteries if his first attested Athenian disciple from Mars Hill (Areopagus) was Dionysus the Areopagite (Acts 17:34), possibly an initiate like much of the Athenian aristocracy. Christianity was not necessarily that similar to the multiple cultic mysteries (others included Dionysian and Samothracian and the Oriental mysteries like Isis, Kybele and Mithras), but Paul may have been appealing to that somewhat competing impulse since they also provided community, salvific experience and something at times like afterlife hope, especially the Eleusinian Mysteries.

The idea of "first fruit" is also found first in the Eleusinian Mysteries long antedating the biblical texts where ἀπαρχὴ "first fruit" is part of the vocabulary of grain harvest the goddesses Demeter and Persephone produced and blessed. Therefore, both Paul's extended grain metaphor and his use of "first fruit" in I Corinthians 15:36-44 would likely make immediate sense to Eleusinian initiates privately and public participants in the Demeter and Kore Sanctuary in Corinth. We already know Paul quotes or alludes to Greek poetry like Aratus' *Phaenomena* and Hellenistic philosophy in his sermon on Mars Hill.[57] For those who still doubt Paul's awareness of Greek culture and philosophy, N. T. Wright's magisterial biography of Paul demonstrates Paul's broad knowledge of Greek philosophy, Plato, Stoicism, Epicureanism and the Cynics.[58] It is not a stretch to assume Paul also had more than a smattering of Greek religion, which he attests on Mars Hill in Acts

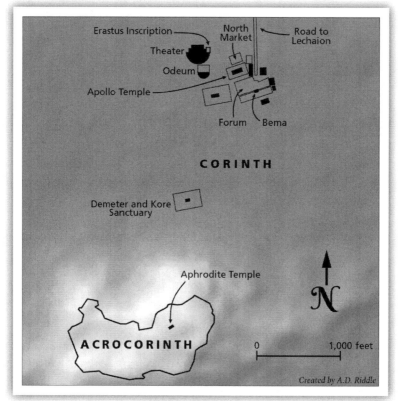

Roman Corinth, 1st c. CE

17 when he states he understood how religious Athenians were, even though the philosophers on Mars Hill would be more skeptical even though so many aristocrats were Eleusinian initiates. Even Socrates and Plato allude to Eleusinian afterlife judges in his *Apologia*.[59]

In conclusion, the Pauline epistle of I Corinthians makes more than a few references to local traditions including its bronze working famous since early antiquity, the consumption of food sacrificed to idols, possibly from Demeter and Kore sacrifices, cultic practices of Demeter and Kore, the carnality of Corinth—the Greek verb *Korinthiazesthai* even meant "to fornicate" and carouse as in Corinth[60]—and the ecstatic or mantic speech of multiple regional Greek oracles near Corinth. That Paul likely attended the Isthmian

Games, carefully discussed since the Classical Greek scholar Oscar Broneer, and furthermore that the Erastus Pavement of the Corinth Theater is to be associated with the Erastus of Romans 16:23 are also corroborating evidences of the textual and archaeological historicity of I Corinthians.

❖

Endnotes Chapter 8

1 Strabo, *Geography* 8.6.20; Lionel Casson, *Travel in the Ancient World.* London: Allen and Unwin, 1979, 91-92.

2 Wayne Meeks, *The First Urban Christians.* New Haven: Yale University Press, 1983, 48-49.

3 Donald Engels, *Roman Corinth: An Alternative Model for a Classical City.* Chicago: University of Chicago Press, 1990, 51 with Beaufort Force 6 wind strength.

4 T. J. Dunbabin, "The Early History of Corinth," *Journal of Hellenic Studies* 68 (1948), 59-69, esp. 59.

5 Nancy Bookidis, "The Sanctuaries of Corinth," *Corinth*, vol. 20. Princeton: American School of Classical Studies, Athens, 2003, 247.

6 Strabo, *Geography* 12.4.36.

7 Pindar, *Fragment* 122s (Snell) *skolion*; see A. P. Burnett, "Servants of Peitho: Pindar fr.122 S," *Greek, Roman, Byzantine Studies* 51 (2011), 49-60.

8 Amy Smith and Sadie Pickup, eds., *Brill's Companion to Aphrodite.* Leiden: E. J. Brill, 2010, 245.

9 Brian S. Rosner, "Temple Prostitution in I Corinthians 6:12-20," *Novum Testamentum* 40.4 (1998), 336-51.

10 Alexandra Villing, Marianne Bergeron, Giorgos Bourogiannis, Alan Johnston, François Leclère, Aurélia Masson, and Ross Thomas, *Naukratis: Greeks in Egypt*, "The Material Culture at Naukratis: An Overview," British Museum (https://research.britishmuseum.org/pdf/Naukratis_ORC_Material_Culture_Villing_Bergeron_Johnston_Masson_Thomas.pdf), 10.

11 J. N. Coldstream, *Geometric Greece: 900-700 BC.* London: Routledge, 2003, 2nd ed., 195.

12 Saul S. Weinberg, "The Geometric and Orientalizing Pottery," *Corinth*, vol. 7.1. Princeton: American School of Classical Studies, Athens (1943), pp. i-xiv, 1-104; Keith De Vries, "Eighth-Century Corinthian Pottery: Evidence for the Dates of Greek Settlement in the West," *Corinth*, vol. 20. Princeton: American School of Classical Studies, Athens, 2003, 141-56.

13 Jerome Murphy O'Connor, "Corinthian Bronze," *Revue Biblique* 90 (1983) 80-91; Carol C. Mattusch. "Corinthian Bronze—famous but elusive," *Corinth*, vol. 20. Princeton: American School of Classical Studies, Athens, 2003, 219-32.

14 Carol C. Mattusch, *Greek Bronze Statuary: From the Beginnings Through the Fifth Century BC.* Ithaca, NY: Cornell University Press, 1988, 71, 90, 98, 221-30; Carol C. Mattusch. *Classical Bronzes: Art and Craft of Greek and Roman Statuary.* Ithaca, NY: Cornell University Press, 1996, 95-6.

15 Pliny, *Hist. Nat.* 34.1-8 & ff., Cicero, *Tusculanae Disputationes*, 4. 32; Plutarch, *Moralia, De Pythiae oraculis* 2 (395b).

16 Ralph Jackson, British Museum, (pers. comm., 2005) and Ralph Jackson, *Doctors and Diseases in the Roman Empire.* London: British Museum Press, 1991; Seth Holmes, "Dyeing Bronze: New Evidence for an Old Reading of *Agamemnon* 612," *Classical Quarterly* 62.2 (2012) 486-95; Susan La Niece and Paul Craddock. *Metal Plating and Patination: Cultural, Technical and Historical developments.* Blackwell/Elsevier, 2017.

17 D. M. Jacobson and M. P. Weitzmann, "What Was Corinthian Bronze?" *American Journal of Archaeology* 96.2 (1992), 237-47.

18 David A. Scott, "The Deterioration of Gold Alloys and Some Aspects of Their Conservation," *Studies in Conservation* 28.4 (1983), 194-203. In an Institute of Archaeology, London, 1987, course in 'Metallography of Ancient Metals' taught by David A. Scott, we viewed a range of corrosion products—including bronze, silver and gold alloys under microscopic analysis. Also note Patrick

Hunt, "Bronze Tabulae Ansatae at Roman Summus Poeninus in the Roman Alps," *Acta II, From the Parts to the Whole: XIIIth International Bronze Congress Proceedings 1996*, vol. 2. Harvard University Art Museums, *Journal of Roman Archaeology Supplement*, 2002. Our Stanford Alpine Archaeology Project 2003 season excavation found a Roman silver coin hoard in a Roman road *mansio* at Plan de Barasson (CH) near the summit of the Grand St-Bernard Pass. Patrick Hunt, "Roman Mansio, Plan de Barasson," *Vallesia* LIV : Recherches Archeologiques dans le Canton du Valais, ed. Francois Wible (1999), 300-8.

19 David M. Jacobson, "Corinthian Bronze and the Gold of the Alchemists," *Gold Bulletin* 33.2 (2000), 60-66.

20 Flavius Josephus, *Wars of the Jews* 5.201

21 Metropolitan Museum of Art, New York, Gallery 137, MMNY Acc. # 19.5

22 Metropolitan Museum of Art, New York, MMNY Acc. # 13.225.5a, b

23 Greek Bronze Cymbals #13.225.5a, b. *Heilbrunn Timeline of Art History*, Metropolitan Museum, New York (https://www.metmuseum.org/toah/works-of-art/13.225.5a,b/).

24 L. H. Peterson, *The Places of Roman Isis: Between Egyptomania, Politics and Religion.* Oxford Handbooks. Oxford: Oxford University Press, 2016.

25 D. E. Smith, "The Egyptian Cults at Corinth," *Harvard Theological Review* 70.3/4 (1977), 201-31, esp. 201-2.

26 Apuleius, *Metamorphosis (Golden Ass)* 11; also described by Pausanias at Cenchreae, *Travels in Greece*, 2.2.3.

27 W. Harris, "Sounding Brass and Hellenistic Technology," *Biblical Archaeology Review* 8.1 (1982); J. Murphy O'Connor, 1983, 80-91; W. W. Klein, "Noisy Gong or Acoustic Vase?" *New Testament Studies* 32 (1986), 286-9; Ben Witherington. *Conflict and Community in*

Corinth: A Socio-Rhetorical Commentary on 1 and 2 Corinthians. Grand Rapids MI: Eerdmans, 1995, 10, 267; Gordon Fee, *First Epistle to the Corinthians* (rev. ed.). Grand Rapids: Eerdmans, 2014, 700.

28 H. G. Liddell and R. Scott, *A Greek-English Lexicon.* Oxford: Clarendon Press (1996 rev.), *chalkokrotou* 1974.

29 Diane Arnson Svarlien, *Pindar Isthmean.* (1990), also *The Odes of Pindar*, in Perseus Project 1.0 (Yale University Press, 1991); *(https:www.* perseus.tufts.edu/hopper/text?).

30 W. H. Race, *Pindar: Nemean Odes, Isthmian Odes, Fragments.* Loeb Classics, Cambridge: Harvard University Press, 1997, 197.

31 Andrew Barker, *Greek Musical Writings I: The Musician and His Art.* Cambridge: Cambridge University Press, 1989 ed., 76, 279.

32 Iulii Pollucis, *Onomasticon*, vol. I (ed. W. Dindorf) Leipzig: Libraria Kuehniana, 1824, 103-4, 436; cf. *chalkion* in Liddell and Scott, *Greek Lexicon* (1996 rev.) 1973.

33 Philip Bosman, "The Dodona Bronze Revisited," *Acta Classica* LIX (2016) 184-92, esp. 184-5.

34 *krotos* (*krotos podon*) from Heraclas Medicus 783 and in the verb *kroteo* (*kroteta pektidon mele*) from Idomeneus *Fragment* 241, both in Liddell and Scott, *Greek Lexicon* 1996 rev., 999.

35 Nancy Bookidis and Ronald Stroud, *Demeter and Persephone in Ancient Corinth.* Princeton: American School of Classical Studies, Athens, 1967.

36 Gloria Merker, *The Sanctuary of Demeter and Kore: Terracotta Figurines of the Classical, Hellenistic and Roman Periods. Corinth*, vol. 18, Princeton: American School of Classical Studies, Athens, 2000, 120, 124, 250-55, 265-6, 277, 298, 327, 340, etc. Note terracotta votive figurines with pigs, e.g., Corinth Arch. Mus., Inv. #MF-10325; Corinth Arch. Mus., Inv. # MF-11785.

37 Nancy Bookidis, Julie Hansen, Lynn Snyder and Paul Goldberg, "Dining in the Sanctuary of Demeter and Kore at Corinth," *Hesperia: Journal of the American School of Classical Studies at Athens* 66.1 (1999), 1-54, esp. 1-2ff"; C. K. Barrett. "Things sacrificed to Idols." *NTS* 11.2 (1964-5) 138-53, on insecure ancient food supply. Also note the relevant Ph.D. dissertation of D. Newton: Derek Newton. "Food offered to Idols in I Corinthians 8-10: A Study of Conflicting Viewpoints in the Setting of Religious Pluralism in Corinth." Sheffield, 1995, esp. 54-59.

38 Note as evidence, for example, the Roman marble piglet votive statue (40 cm length) in Pentelic Marble at the Eleusis Archaeological Museum, Inv. # 5053.

39 Liddell and Scott, *Greek Lexicon*, 1996 ed., *glossa* as "language" in II, 353.

40 I. J. Martin, "Glossalalia in the Apostolic Church," *Journal of Biblical Literature* 63.2 (1944), 123-30.

41 L. Carlyle May, "A Survey of Glossalalia and Related Phenomena in Non-Christian Religions," *American Anthropologist* (NS) 58.1 (1956), 75-96; James D. G. Dunn. *Jesus and the Spirit.* SCM Press, 1975; Christopher Forbes. "Early Christian Inspired Speech and Hellenistic Popular Religion," *Novum Testamentum* XXXVIII.3 (1986), 257-70.

42 Diodorus Siculus, *Bibliotheke Historia* 4.66.6-7.

43 Forbes, 257; e.g., *Aeneid* 6.80, 100, 102: *os rabidum*, "raving or frenzied mouth" line 80; *obscuris vera involvens*, "wrapping truths in darkness" in line 100; *rabida ora*, "raving lips or mouth" in line 102. cf. Clyde Pharr, *Vergil's Aeneid Books I-VI.* Lexington, MA: D. C. Heath, rev. ed. 1964, 310-13.

44 Joseph Fontenrose, *Python: A Study of Delphic Myth and Its Origins.* Berkeley: University of California Press, 1980;

45 Witherington, 267.

46   Martina Dieterle, *Dodona*. Spudasmata Bd. 116. Hildesheim: G. Olms, 2007; Martina Dieterle, "Dodona," in *Blackwell-Wiley Encyclopedia of the Ancient World*, 2012.

47   Albert Schachter, "A Boeotian Cult Type," *Bulletin of the Institute of Classical Studies* 14 (1967), 1-16, esp. 9; Raymond J. Clark. "Trophonios: the Manner of His Revelation." *Transactions and Proceedings of the American Philological Association* 99 (1968) 63-75.

48   Emily Pillinger, *Cassandra and the Poetics of Prophecy in Greek and Latin Literature*. Cambridge: Cambridge University Press, 2019, 30ff..

49   H. W. Parke, *The Oracles of Zeus*. Oxford: Blackwell, 1967.

50   Scholia glosses on Aristophanes, *Peace*, 1070; on *Birds*, 962; Matthew Dillon. *Omens and Oracles: Divination in Ancient Greece*. London: Routledge, 2017, 34-35.

51   Judith Swaddling, *Olympic Games*. London: British Museum Press, 2001 repr.

52   Oscar Broneer, "The Corinthian Isthmus and the Isthmian Sanctuary," *Antiquity* 32.126 (1958), 80-88; Oscar Broneer, "The Apostle Paul and then Isthmian Games." *Biblical Archeologist* 25.1 (1962) 1-31.

53   F. F. Bruce, *The Epistle to the Hebrews*. Grand Rapids: Eerdmans, 1975, 6th pr., xxxix-xl, 108, 269, 274, 349ff.

54   John Harvey Kent, *Corinth VIII, Part III, The Inscriptions 1926-50*, Princeton: American School of Classical Studies, Athens, 1966, esp. 99-100; Anthony C. Thistleton, *The First Epistle to the Corinthians*. Grand Rapids: Eerdmans, 2013, 9.

55   Kent, *ibid.*

56   George Mylonas, *Eleusis and the Eleusinian Mysteries*. Princeton: Princeton University Press, 1961, 242; C. Kerenyi. *Eleusis: Archetypal Image of Mother and Daughter*. Princeton: Princeton University Press, 1967.

57 N. Clayton Croy, "Hellenistic Philosophies and the Preaching of the Resurrection (Acts 17:18, 32)," *Novum Testamentum* 39.1 (1997), 21-39; also D. A. Akenson, Saint Saul: *A Skeleton Key to the Historical Jesus.* Oxford: Oxford University Press, 2002, 155, where Paul encountered problems of "syncretistic alliances with pagan religions" in Corinth.

58 N. T. Wright, *Paul: A Biography.* New York: Harper, 2018, 16-17. Also note the excellent new study of Laura S. Nasrallah. *Archaeology and the Letters of Paul.* Oxford: Oxford University Press, 2019, 22, as archaeology now aids in "understand[ing] Christianity as emerging among multiple cults."

59 Plato, *Apologia* 32; Patrick Hunt, "Triptolemos and Beyond in the Stanford Kleophon Krater," *Stanford Museum Journal,* 2001, 3-8.

60 A. N. Wilson, *Paul: The Mind of the Apostle.* New York: W. W. Norton and Co. 1997, 161.

9

The Throne of Charlemagne: Carolingian and Biblical Symbolism and Archaeology

❖

Charlemagne's Throne, Aachen Cathedral, ca. 800 (Photo P. Hunt 2019)

Aachen Cathedral (also known in German as the *Kaiserdom*) is one of the most important monuments in the Early Medieval world, begun circa 796, and symbolically identified with the end of the Dark Ages when literacy was finally resurgent in the Carolingian Age. According to Einhard, his posthumous biographer, Charlemagne built Aachen's Palatine Church and adjacent palace:

Hence it was that he built his palace at Aachen, and lived there constantly during his latter years until his death…He built the beautiful basilica at Aachen, which he adorned with gold and silver and lamps, and with rails and doors of solid brass. He had the columns and marbles for this structure brought from Rome and Ravenna, for he could not find such as were suitable elsewhere.[1]

Revisiting in March 2019, the author spent more time than previously, especially studying the throne identified with Charlemagne, the *Karlsthron* in German, also named the *Aachener Königsthron* and identified with coronation of German emperors until 1531. Whether it was constructed before or after Charlemagne's own imperial coronation in Old St. Peter's Basilica of Rome in 800 by Pope Leo III is uncertain. Whether he could have been re-crowned in this throne later in his reign subsequent to 796 as King or Imperator of the Franks is also unknown.

Constructed of four simple cream-hued marble slabs joined by bronze straps or clamps (p. 129), its provenance and history are much conflated by legend rather than known facts, but even some of the conjectural history is not only fascinating but highly relevant to Charlemagne himself and subsequent imperial authority. Aachen Palatine Cathedral's upper gallery (west side) is approached by a staircase from the ground level, and there the throne has its private location in the hexagonal basilica—built and decorated in Byzantine style as the architectural canons of the Carolingian Era demanded. Although now somewhat stripped bare of accouterments, including the wooden seat likely covered in fabric, the throne is elevated on a limestone platform and fitted with six marble steps (derived from quartered columns) that is likely also an allegory of biblical Solomon's throne—approached by six steps as I Kings 10:18-19 (NRSV) states: "The king [Solomon] also made a great ivory throne, and overlaid it with the finest gold. The throne had six steps. The top of the throne was rounded in the back…"

Although a clear difference is that Solomon's throne was said to be made of ivory and covered in gold in this biblical literary account, Charlemagne's is marble, an important distinction discussed in

*Thronus Solomonis from Darmstradt Speculum
ms. 2505 19 recto side, ca. 1360
(courtesy of Universitäts und Landesbibliothek Darmstadt)*

following paragraphs as this marble is legendary and possibly more "precious" than ivory. Like Solomon's, this throne has a rounded back. Note the circa 1360 Medieval image above of King Solomon on his throne from the *Speculum Darmstadt* ms 2505 19r Westfalen (Universitäts- und Landesbibliothek Darmstadt) with six steps and rounded back (is this medieval depiction derived from the Karlsthron in Aachen or the description from I Kings 10:19? (see photo on p. 131). The Latin below the illumination declares it as *Thronus Solomonis.*

While it would have been necessary to add a lowest black marble step to make six steps to solidify an allusion to King Solomon—this deliberation is emphasized by the fact that five are pale marble and one is black marble—the symbolic yet visceral connection to Solomon as the richest and wisest ruler of biblical history would have only further elevated the legend of Charlemagne.

A narrow interior hollow space under the Karlsthron's marble slabs is polished from many visitors (including the most distinguished royalty of Europe) crawling through over a millennium, although now chained off from the public who can walk around the throne.

The throne sits on an original platform (see photo on p. 133) of colored decorative stones in *opus sectile* historically connected to Roman Imperium.[2] Mostly identified with Roman emperors such as Trajan and Hadrian at Rome's zenith in the early second century CE, these semiprecious and expensive stones are rarely found together except in the most important Roman buildings like the Pantheon in Rome (hence Einhard's above comment in *Vita Caroli Magni* 26 that stones for the church were brought from Rome and Ravenna).[3] These Karlsthron platform *opus sectile* decorative stones are: a) *Imperial Porphyry* (or *Porfido Rosso)* (purple) from Mons Porphyrites or Gebel Dokhan in Egypt—the most expensive stone in Diocletian's *Price Edict* in 301 CE; b) *Lapis Lacedaemonius* (or *Porfido Verde*), Spartan Green Porphyry (green with phenocrysts and sometimes bearing even amethyst crystals); c) *Giallo Numidiana* (or *Giallo Antico*), Royal Carthaginian marble from Mt. Chemtou in Tunisia in what was Ancient Punic Carthage (cream yellow with burgundy streaked intrusions); d) *Docimian Pavonozetto* or "Peacock" Marble from Asia Minor (white with purple streaked intrusion; and e) *Granito Bigio,* a gray granite possibly from a yet-unknown source.[4] All these Roman imperial stones are found in the Hadrianic Pantheon—the *Porfido verde* banded on the wall rather than on the pavement—circa 125, (see photo on p. 134), unlikely to be coincidental given Charlemagne's status as new *Imperator Romanorum* (did his court acquire these stones in 800 during his coronation journey?).

Charlemagne's Throne Platform in Opus Sectile
(Photo P. Hunt 2019)

Pantheon (Rome) opus sectile Pavement of same
decorative stone as Aachen (Photo P. Hunt, 2014)

The six marble steps on the throne platform (see photo on
p. 135)—which faces east toward the basilica interior, a possibly important symbolic feature identifying the relative direction of Jerusalem—
are curved on the underside and four of which were clearly carved from
a quartered column (or columns) most likely Roman in origin; although
the column pieces like the marble slabs could be from the Church of the
Holy Sepulchre in an earlier phase between periodic destructions and
rebuilding from 335 onward. While legend has at some time connected
the marble steps to Pilate's Roman court in Jerusalem, it is at present
impossible to prove such a legend since the Praetorium court (whether
Herod's Palace or Antonia Fortress—most archaeologists favor Herod's
Palace) is long gone since around 70 CE with Jerusalem's destruction by
Rome. Possible marble provenance will be discussed below.

Karlsthron six steps (mainly five whitish marble steps are easily visible)
(Photo P. Hunt, 2019)

Perhaps the most intriguing questions about Charlemagne's Throne concern the origin of its plain marble slabs. Tradition and even modern scholarship maintain they are from the Church of the Holy Sepulchre of Jerusalem.[5] This remains unproven but the symbolism is profound even if the marble is not truly from Jerusalem. A first caveat is that marble is not found in Israel even if local Cenomanian Limestone can be fairly highly polished, so if the throne slabs are marble, the source must come from the Hellenistic or Roman occupations of Jerusalem. Tradition with fairly consistent documentation holds that Helena, mother of Constantine, established the original Church of the Holy Sepulchre on or adjacent to the Golgotha Crucifixion site in late 335 with the help of Bishop Eusebius of Caesarea and Bishop Macarius of Jerusalem. So any stone remnants from that Golgotha association truly would be sacred to

Christendom. Proving this physical connection is immensely difficult given the vicissitudes of destruction on the site over subsequent millennia. Determining the stone material used in the 4th c. building is problematic. Emperor Hadrian in renaming Jerusalem as *Aelia Capitolina* after his family name (*Aelius*), had built a temple to Jupiter or Venus circa 135 CE over Golgotha hill and filled in the quarry. Presumably marble would have been used for such Roman temple construction, so that Roman marble material may be the source. Much subsequent damage prior to Charlemagne in the interim between the 4th and late 8th centuries could account for reused Roman rubble reclaimed by the Byzantine Orthodox prelates, although Helena could have obtained marble fragments from either or both Eusebius or Macarius since Caesarea and Jerusalem had ample Roman structures of marble.

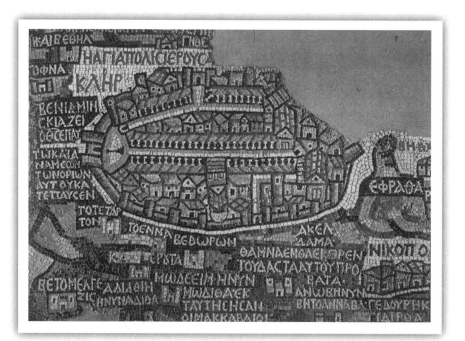

Madaba Mosaic Map, mid-6th c. Madaba, Jordan
(image on public domain)

The Madaba Mosaic Map of the 6th century CE (see photo on p. 136) definitely depicts the Church of the Holy Sepulchre centered on Jerusalem's west side facing east to the Cardo Maximus with its Rotunda dome. By this time the Christian site comprised at least three structures: the *Martyrium* basilica, the colonnaded *Atrium Triportico* and the *Anastasis* Rotunda (as mentioned, the last of which architecture appears to be the westernmost unit on the Madaba Map depiction). So, the church was recognizably intact from the time of Helena until at least the mid-6th c., although fire destroyed much of Jerusalem ostensibly including the church when the Persian Sassanid King Khosrau II invaded in 614 CE. The church was documented as rebuilt in 630 by the Byzantine Emperor Heraclius, although again suffering severe damage by earthquake in 746, after which point the Carolingians likely would not have easily obtained any such fragments as to be carefully provenanced and ultimately brought to Aachen during the building of its cathedral under Charlemagne. Essentially from even before the Carolingian Period until the Crusades (long after Charlemagne), Jerusalem was greatly under the control of Islam and the marble materials would not be so easily obtained as during the earliest period of Constantine and Helena.

Many related questions about the marble slabs are unanswerable but nonetheless relevant for symbolic reasons. If the Karlsthron material is indeed Roman marble, does it come from Hadrian's temple over the filled in site, then procured as rubble from the visit of Helena? Was the previous Roman rubble material including marble taken to Rome under Helena's reliquary search (including fragments of the "True Cross") or later to Ravenna and obtained by Charlemagne during his coronation visit in 800? (see Helena legend photo on p. 138). Constantine had already ordered the Hadrianic Capitolinus removed from what had been Golgotha in 327 so that Roman rubble—or was it too desecrated?—was available for the building of the Church of the Holy Sepulchre and pragmatics often held sway in reusing old stone rather than quarrying new stone; geologic indigenous marble was as mentioned not found in Palestine in any case. Eusebius (*Life of Constantine* 26-27) notes the overlying Roman rubble was removed under Constantine's orders in the search for the Tomb of Jesus; following this, Eusebius relates how

Constantine commanded the building of the Church of the Holy Sepulchre with polished stone and adornments (*Life of Constantine* 30-32), no doubt also importing new marble. On the one hand, it seems unlikely the Byzantine religious powers would let slip from their possession marbles perceived as possible relics of the Roman crucifixion.

One of the considerable problems with this scenario of moving rubble marble to Rome is that Constantine had already moved his capital to Constantinople by 330, so why would the marble go to Italy (like the proverbial "coals to Newcastle") instead of Constantinople? On the

Helena Legend Rondel with "True Cross" Miracles, Stavelot
"True Cross" Triptych, 12th c. J. P. Morgan Library
(Photo P. Hunt, 2018)

South Side Slab of Karlsthron with inscribed Roman game Merellus
("Nine Man's Morris") (Photo P. Hunt, 2019)

other hand, Justinian's building program in Ravenna, could explain such a transfer to Italy around 540. Ravenna was the capital of the Western Roman Empire from 402-76, then the Ostrogoth capital until 540 when Byzantium conquered it, and remained a Byzantine exarchate even after the Langobards came, although the Langobards were defeated by Charlemagne in 774. The partial rebuilding of Christian Rome after the Ostrogoths could suggest these Roman rubble slabs—perceived as relics from Jerusalem—could then go to Rome.

Another fascinating feature on the south throne slab is the incised game known by the Romans as *merellus* and later as Nine Men's Morris (above). *Merellus* Glass game pieces (or *merella*) are prolific—the author has excavated quite a few even from obscure remote Roman sites such as the high altitude Roman mansio below *Summus Poeninus* in the Pennine Alps (Great St. Bernard Pass) (see photo on p. 140).[6]

Perhaps vitally important to Charlemagne and his artists, the Roman *merellus* game inscribed on the Karlsthron might have been interpreted as the very spot (however unlikely) where Roman soldiers gambled for the garments Jesus possessed that the gospels note (e.g. Matthew 27:35) were divided by throwing game pieces. These marble slabs would then be even more important relics if thus connected, however dubious in actual fact (pious onlookers could point out: "Look, here is where our Lord's very garments were divided under the Cross"). Would Rome's and/or Ravenna's prelates offer these very same marble spolia fragments to Charlemagne in 800 to solidify his being *Imperator Romanorum* with a spiritually-invested Christlike kingship? Coronation on the Throne of Charlemagne for subsequent rulers was necessarily "touching" and grounded by such relics.[7]

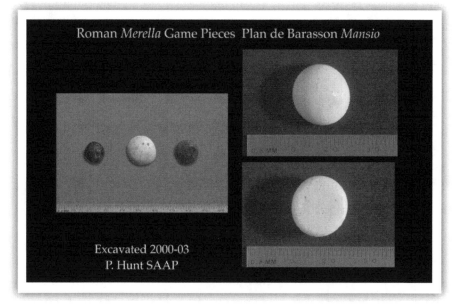

Roman Glass merella game pieces (exc. 2000-03) from Roman Mansio below Summus Poeninus, now in ORA Martigny (Photo P. Hunt, 2000-03)

Again, because these provenance questions cannot be easily answered and while such conjecture cannot really be proven, it is critical to remember that perception so often transcended fact and could be more important: it is the symbolic nature of such "relics" that provide Christological propaganda and imperial power to the builders and purveyors of such Carolingian legend, something Charlemagne would have greatly appreciated, with these powerful relics to bolster his very throne.

Thus Charlemagne's claim could rest on a perceived *imperium* derived from some of the holiest relics in Christendom: alluding Solomon's Throne as the seat of wisdom, perceived slabs from the Church of the Holy Sepulchre, indeed even an inscribed Roman board game seemingly alluding to Christ's crucifixion spot, all cement his authority as Holy Roman Emperor. Even if none of these are provable, their perceptual power was politically appropriated. Such is the power of perception that all of this purported provenance could be false and yet the biblical symbolism would be just as powerful for the Carolingian Age if people thought these were true architectural artifacts of Christ's crucifixion and tomb, more symbolically powerful than a trove of many other possible saintly relics.

❖

Endnotes Chapter 9

1   Einhard, *Vita Caroli Magni* 22, 26.

2   Patrick Hunt, "Pantheon" in *Encyclopedia of the Ancient World.* Salem Press, 2002, 868. Also see Patrick Hunt, "Imperium and Genius in the Pantheon of Rome," *Electrum Magazine,* May, 2016 (http://www.electrummagazine.com/2016/05/imperium-and-genius-in-the-pantheon-of-rome/).

3   Amanda Claridge, *Rome: Oxford Archaeological Guides.* Oxford University Press, 1998 (2010 printing), 201-7, esp. 206 & 226-33.

4   Luisa Carlei, Simonetta de Felicis Orlandi, Paola Ferraris, Maria Cristina Marhei and Gabriele Borghini, eds, *Marmi Antichi.* Rome: Edizione de Luca, 1997. Note pp. 214-5 (*Giallo Numidiana* or *Giallo antico*); pp. 218-9 (*Granito Bigio* varieties, possibly from Algeria, Egypt or Pyrenees?); p. 264 (*Docimian Pavonazetto* or *Marmor Phrygium*); p. 274 (Imperial Porphyry or *Porfido Rosso*); p. 279 (*Lapis Lacedaemonius* or *Porfido Verde).*

5   Konstantin Klein, "Wo Josephine sich einst verkohlte" (Karlsthron). Archäologische Kolloquium, Universität Bamberg May 15, 2007. Summarizing the research of archaeologist Dr. Sven Schütte, who established that the original Karlsthron wood seat dates to 800, the same time as Charlemagne's coronation journey to Rome. Schütte also underscores the similarity of this hued marble to that of the Holy Sepulchre, including the divided column that became the throne stairs. Also see Sven Schütte, "Der Aachener Thron," in M. Kramp (Ed.): *Krönungen, Könige in Aachen—Geschichte und Mythos.* Verlag Philipp von Zabern, 1999, 213–222.

6   Patrick Hunt, "Summus Poeninus on the Great Bernard Pass," *Journal of Roman Archaeology* XI (1998), 264ff.

7   Klein notes: "According to Schütte, it was of fundamental impor-tance for the kings who were crowned on the [Karls]throne to be "connected" with the material." Also note Herta Lepie and Georg Minkenberg, *The Cathedral Treasury of Aachen,* Schnell—Steiner,

Regensburg, 2013, 2nd ed. 64-5 where the coronation on Charlemagne's Throne of 30 kings and 12 queens was directly associated with holy relics and their assumed power and sanctity from 936-1541.

10

The Four Horsemen of the Apocalypse in Revelation 6 and History

❖

*Albrecht Dürer's "The Four Horesemen of the Apocalypse" ca. 1497/98,
The Metropolitan Museum of Art (Image in public domain)*

What are the "Four Horsemen of the Apocalypse"? Famine, disease, war and death is the simple and common answer but their compounded interrelationships must also be considered. Too many futuristically interpret Revelation 6:1-6 solely as prophecy when this passage actually references cyclical history, a scenario repeated untold times over many human millennia, likely in fairly frequent intervals through the Holocene over the last 11,700 years or more. Of course, this textual sequence can always be prophetic too, not just looking backward but forward, because these concatenated cycles will return again and again. In the biblical passage Revelation 6:1-4 describes war, and the verses of Revelation 6:7-8 describe disease and death. Sometimes these catastrophes are individual and not connected in a cyclical sequence because they can often happen singly as well. Closely examining the single most detailed excerpt of the "Four Horsemen" we can start with famine in Revelation 6:5-6. Famine itself can be caused by preceding multiple factors, unlikely to be fully understood in antiquity, but the outcome is clear in the text:

> "When the Lamb opened the third seal, I heard the third living creature say, "Come!" I looked, and there before me was a black horse! Its rider was holding a pair of scales in his hand. Then I heard what sounded like a voice among the four living creatures, saying, "A quart of wheat for a day's wages, and three quarts of barley for a day's wages, and do not damage the oil and the wine!" Revelation 6:5-6

The above famine segment of the Apocalypse Cycle is notable in this excerpt. For comparison, a full "day's wage" in any era might equal around $150 by modern standards, although this is not necessarily applicable to antiquity. Such a daily wage ~$150 assumes an average reported U.S. annual wage in 2017 of $56,000 according to U.S. Census Bureau divided by 12 months divided by 30 days = ~$155). Therefore if $155 is needed for only a quart of wheat (~2 lbs.), the marked scarcity of food and its high cost is highlighted. The above text uses the Roman *denarius* (δηναρίου in the Greek dative case: "for a denarius") as a day's wage at the time of writing. The metaphorical symbol of weighing commodities in this passage is the balance scale where one thing is weighed against another, hence a pair of scales. Comparing the value of wheat against barley is also a useful economic detail of famine, where at the time of writing in the Roman Era, wheat might appear to be three times more valuable than barley. But here, since the text doesn't give a value for a day's wages, a reader in antiquity would still acknowledge the effect of famine in very high food cost for a standard food staple. The above text may not spell out famine by using it as a word here, but it is clearly the predicament described in the narrative of Revelation 6:5-6.

As suggested, the causal background of this Apocalypse Cycle (famine, disease, war and death) is complex because these catastrophes are often interrelated. Often due to climatic perturbations, crop failure and diminished food supply lead to famine, followed by pestilence or plague when malnutrition leads to compromised immune systems, followed by chaos and civil war as societies cannot maintain control, with balance spiraling out of hand, followed by death. Sometimes the latter two "Horsemen of the Apocalypse" as seen War and Death are out of sequence or skipping a full cycle, but generally the first two, famine and plague are in necessary tandem. While the full cycle can be easily viewed in Medieval Europe with the Black Death circa 1346-53, beginning with the Great Famine in 1314-17,[1] it can be readily apparent in many other times of history as well including in Reformation Europe,[2] and many other times before and after, including in 537-40 CE as described by Procopius when Constantinople and the Byzantine world were affected.[3]

Plague and disease data—extrapolated from epidemiology studies in the modern world and paleopathology in the ancient world[4]--rarely are available as corroborated by taphonomy, but disease is often discussed as a subsequent phase after famine in the Apocalypse Cycle. The main consequence of famine, if not outright starvation and death therefrom, is malnutrition from diminished food supply. Malnutrition also leads to compromised immune systems, exactly when infectious disease attacks weakened bodies where resistance is already moot.

This Apocalypse Cycle also helps to explain some of the distinctions and breaks between Bronze and Iron Ages and their internal subdivisions such as Old, Middle, and Late Bronze Ages; Iron I, II, etc. The idea of Stone Age, Bronze Age, Iron Age chronologies were originally devised by Christian Jürgensen Thomsen, (1788-1865), in his *Ledetraad til Nordisk Oldkyndighed*, 1848, and while primarily based on the material usage changes from stone to bronze to iron,[5] we can also often divide these periods and a frequent hiatus between them by the apocalypses and cultural collapses. It is now noteworthy that these basic periods chronologically parallel the climate perturbations reflected in the pollen record when drought was manifest with low pollen count preserved.[6] The dating of time periods through materials by stylistic changes in artifacts, especially ceramics, architecture, weapons, art, etc., shows distinct times when cultures and civilizations wane and fail, with cessation of recognizable activities, followed by dormancy or absence of materials, then new cultures rise up with their own distinctive hallmarks. It is now generally accepted that the end of the Early Bronze Age was synchronous in Egypt's Old Kingdom as well from Mesopotamian climate change that ended Akkadian dominance and also affected Egypt.[7]

Several recent authors who have detailed these often cataclysmic changes include Eric Cline and Ian Morris, both eminent archaeologists and ancient historians (and at one time or another, Stanford colleagues). Morris wrote the seminal work *Why The West Rules—For Now* (2010) and Eric Cline wrote *1177 BC: The Year Civilization Collapsed* (2014), both variations on the theme of apocalypse.[8] Morris introduces migration as a non-textual fifth horseman, either driven by the other four or compounding them. I first formulated the famine aspect of the Four Horsemen in 2009 in a Stanford lecture and website,[9] but have revisited it here to illustrate how disastrous multiple sequential years of famine can cripple civilizations.

To better understand how the Apocalypse Cycle can be set in motion by famine, grain harvests are important. We know from Nilotic inundation records and even better from Chinese record-keeping of volcanic eruptions in Indonesia, for example, five specific super volcanoes noted in the 14th century as well as millennia of volcanic events[10] that vast amounts of volcanic ash in the atmosphere can cause a chain of climatic events leading to poor harvests, subsequent famine and so on.

Here is a hypothetical scenario from diminishing grain harvest that helps to grasp the results of famine in the principle of diminishing returns: If in a normal grain harvest year, a small farm yield in the ancient world was hypothetically ~100 bushels, then we can assume less in a bad harvest year. Naturally, yield varied per farmer so this number of 100 bushels is completely arbitrary and only used here as a standard against which lower harvests are compared in climatic perturbations. If a good or normal year is followed by a bad year (Y1)—whether due to not enough rainfall (drought) or too much rainfall (flooding)—with only 25% reduction of grain yield to 75 bushels, this wouldn't necessarily heavily impact health. We assume a 10% saving of harvest yield for seed for the next year, but instead of planting 10 bushels for seed from 100 bushels of yield, it would be practical to plant 10% of 75 bushels = 7.5 bushels for seed. But a subsequent bad year (Y2) of either drought of flood with another 25% reduction of harvest might yield only around 56 bushels, in which case 10% (=5.6 bushels) would be saved for seed. Without question, population nutrition would be impacted: same number of mouths to feed including stock

animals but only half the normal food supply. If a third year (Y3) of grain harvest yield was similarly reduced to around 36-40 bushels, the nutrition impact would be even more severe, with malnutrition seriously affecting health, significantly weakening a population and likely leading to loss of resistance to pandemic contagion.

Grain harvest to feed humans and animals with 10% annual seed reserve

This hypothetical scenario, however, does not allow for a possibly more realistic compounding reduction at a greater rate than 25% loss. It is likely the poor, very young and very old would have compromised immune systems and less resilience, with population loss likely faster than population gain if there was little adaptive ability to provide sufficient food resources by another means. In this scenario famine clearly

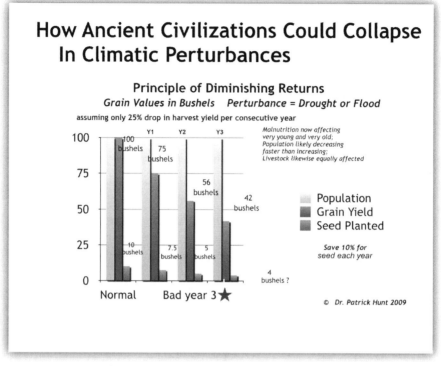

Climatic Perturbation's Effect on Harvest and Famine

sets up a population for disease by weakened overall health. Not only is there less grain to eat and less grain to plant for seed, but there are less healthy workers and less robust animals tasked to farm. This is why a multiple year drought in the ancient world could bring civilizations to their knees, especially if the climatic perturbation extended over a wide enough geographic area that potential short-distance migration was necessary but also contributory to instability, a problem since territoriality usually meant shared resources were unlikely. This is where famine also led to war, with whole populations on the move if disease and death did not strike first.

Such a concatenated catastrophe of natural disasters and poor human response (Cline's "perfect storm") likely brought down the Mycenaean Culture in the Late Bronze Age around 1200 BCE, resulting in, among other instabilities, the migrations of the "Sea Peoples" away from the Aegean a few generations later. Dothan's surveys also showed a once-prosperous Canaan in the Late Bronze that abruptly collapsed around 1200 BCE.[11] Similarly, the migrations of the barbarian waves that left the steppes and reached Roman Europe toward the middle of the 1st millennium CE may have also been partly caused by overpopulation and then diminishing natural resources and agricultural failure in the steppes and Central Asia.[12] Early proponents of climate disasters as part of the fall of Roman Empire—with agricultural failure compounded by soil exhaustion—include Arragon as early as 1932,[13] long before paleo-climatology was accepted in modern scholarly circles as instrumental in cultural collapse. The Roman Empire itself was certainly hit with wild climate fluctuations that contributed to its fall.[14]

It is also well known that the Great Plague of 539-542 in Constantinople and the East Mediterranean directly followed the climate change that was likely caused by vast clouds of Indonesian volcanic ash from Krakatoa and other stratovolcanoes (and a possible comet collision breaking up in earth's atmosphere) in 535 ("the year of no sun when fruit froze on trees" according to Procopius,[15]) and dust that ruined agricultural productivity for several years,[16] all of which quickly led to famine and then plague by 540, all following the same Four Horsemen Apocalypse Cycle even if incomplete. Others who recorded the dire weather of 535 include Michael the Syrian, Priscianus Johannes Lydus in the Byzantine East, and the Anglo-Saxon scholar Gildas in the West.[17] Showing how pervasive the volcanic ash and dust were even in the north, Scandinavians recorded the year 535 as *Fimbulwinter*, "Twilight of the Gods" when the gods shivered in Asgard, itself frozen. Additional bioarchaeology evidence from British Isles dendrochronology in the graph below shows a large drop in tree ring growth in oaks in Belfast (dots) and Whithorn (circles) restricted by diminished solar radiation in the second half of the decade 530-540, especially after 537.[18] Further compounding this 6th century Apocalypse Cycle, British Isles stability took a bit hit with a resulting great famine ending the *Pax Britannia* in the mid 6th c. CE.

One of the last images in this chapter is from the visual plague record of the 14th and 15th c., a phenomenon already discussed ear-lier when severe cold and other climatic perturbations resulted in the

Great Famine of the 14th century (1314-17), followed quickly by malnutrition, loss of immune system resistance to disease, and the great plague of Black Death between 1346-53.

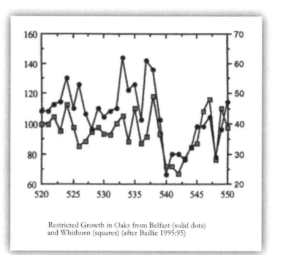

Restricted Growth in Oaks from Belfast (dots) and Whithorn (squares) dendrochronology (after Baillie, 1995)

Again as before, vast volcanic eruptions in Iceland helped precipitate cold weather disasters and famine in Europe in the early 14th century. The Anonymous Master of Death painting in the Palazzo Abbatellis of Palermo, Sicily, shows Death on the pale horse riding across a landscape, shooting arrows into the lymph nodes of the neck of people of all walks of life and social standing. Kings, bishops, sultans and the nobility (trying to entertain themselves as in Boccaccio's *Decameron* during plague) are struck without avail. Fascinating in the painting is the cognition that the plague came from the East: note Death's compound bow associated with the Golden Horde and Mongol Wars.

Judging by her eyes, the aristocratic lady on the lower far right in this detail is just feeling the arrow striking in her neck region. The exceptionally observant anonymous artist may not have yet known lymphatic anatomy and physiology but did record where the resulting fight against infection (whether bubonic or pneumonic) appeared most aggressively on the body.

This graphic Late Medieval/Early Renaissance painting (because Sicily's ports like Palermo would been directly part of the plague transport) thus portrays a realistic grasp of the geographic origin and surges of effects of the 14th century and recurring Black Death that killed off at least 60 % of the total European population (50 million deaths)[19] and

80% or greater in some port cities, and nearly 76% in Tuscan communes such as San Gimignano between 1332-1427 and 76% in Pistoia between 1244-1404,[20] with a full iteration of the Four Horsemen of the Apocalypse Cycle of famine, disease, war and death. As mentioned earlier, plague and the other catastrophes can occur singly outside the cycle, but famine often leads to pandemic plague and death as in the 6th c. and 14th c. CE.

Pale Horse of Death, Anonymous Master of Death, Palermo, Sicily, ca. 1450

In conclusion, while not every ancient recorded climatic perturbation resulted in the full Apocalypse Cycle, the events we can now connect with drought or extreme temperatures and resulting pollen count or tree ring diminution range from the end of the Early Bronze Age and the end of the late Bronze Age to the Late Roman/Early Byzantine terminus as well as the end of the Medieval Period and the Renaissance; many of them in some way associated with volcanic ash and dust and famines and plagues of the 14th century.

Thus, the famous Four Horsemen Apocalypse Cycle of Famine, Disease, War, and Death as portrayed in the Revelation 6 text may not have been recognized as history at the time of writing, but certainly it may be understood now in some way depicting a series of repeated historic events documented since antiquity and evidenced across archaeological disciplines—among them: paleopathology (study of ancient diseases), taphonomics (including chronological studies of grave goods and bones), ceramic technology (including makeup and distribution of pottery), archaeometallurgy (including history of alloys), bioarchaeology (broader biological artifacts including tree rings in dendrochronology), archaeoethnobotany (as recorded in documented crop failure) and palynology (distribution and volume of extant pollen), among other metrics of antiquity. As a textual source for history, the biblical account of concatenated Apocalypse Cycles in Revelation 6 is not only relevant through past events but likely prophetic with natural, not supernatural, repetitions—of future cataclysms. Plus, the obvious connection to archaeology is that these periods of collapse help archaeologists to differentiate time periods by the contrasts in material goods when one cultural period eventually follows another that has ended due to the crises of these Apocalypse Cycles. Such differentiation is usually easily reflected in the changing styles of artifacts found on archaeological sites.

❖

Endnotes Chapter 10

1   William C. Jordan, *The Great Famine: Northern Europe in the Early Fourteenth Century.* Princeton: Princeton University Press, 1996; William Rosen. *The Third Horseman: Climate Change and the Great Famine of the 14th Century.* London: Viking / Penguin, 2014.

2   Andrew Cunningham and Ole Peter Grell, *Religion, War, Famine and Death in Reformation Europe.* Cambridge: Cambridge University Press, 2001.

3   Anthony Kaldellis, ed./tr. *Procopius: The Secret History with Related Texts.* Indianapolis: Hackett, (Wars 2.22-23ff), 164-72; William Rosen, *Justinian's Flea: The First Great Plague and the End of the Roman Empire.* London: Viking/Penguin, 2007, esp. 205-17.

4   Also see Chapter 5 in this book on Sennacherib and paleopathology; C.A. Roberts, "Palaeopathology and its relevance to understanding health and disease today: the impact of the environment on health, past and present," *Anthropological Review* (De Gruyter) 79.1 (2016) 1-16.

5   Bruce Trigger, *A History of Archaeological Thought.* Cambridge University Press, 2006, 2nd ed., 121-38ff.

6   S. Bottema, "Third Millennium Climate Change in the Near East Based upon Pollen Evidence," *Third Millennium B.C. Climate Change and Old World Collapse,* N. Dalfes, G. Kukla, and H. Weiss, eds, NATO ASI Series 1.49. Berlin: Springer Verlag (1997), 489-515.

7   H. M. Cullen, P. B. de Menocal, S. Hemming, G. Hemming, F. H. Brown, T. Guilderson, and F. Sirocko, "Climate Change and the Collapse of the Akkadian Empire: Evidence from the Deep Sea," *Journal of Geology* 28 (2000), 79-382.

8   Ian Morris, *Why The West Rules - For Now.* New York: Farrar, Straus, Giroux, 2010, 297, 455, 564, 576-7 (five horsemen including migration); Eric Cline, *1177 BC: The Year Civilization Collapsed.*

Princeton: Princeton University Press, 2014, esp. 133, 145, 162-3, all part of the "perfect storm".

9   Patrick Hunt, ""Four Horsemen of the Apocalypse: from Paleoclimates to the Present," *Philolog* (Stanford) Jan., 2009 (http://traumwerk.stanford.edu/philolog/2009/02/four_horsemen_of_the_apocalyps.html *original* html but not all these html have transferred to the permanent Stanford servers.)

10 R. Torrence, C. Pavlides, P. Jackson and J. Webb, "Volcanic Disasters and Cultural Discontinuities in Holocene Time in West New Britain, Papua New Guinea," in W. J. McGuire, D. R. Griffiths, P. L. Hancock and I. S. Stewart, eds. *The Archaeology of Geological Catastrophes*. Geological Society Special Publication no. 171. London: Geological Society of London, 2000, 225-44.

11 Cline, 1177 BCE, 122, 145-7, 155-7, 162-3; Trude Dothan and Moshe Dothan, *People of the Sea: The Search for the Philistines*. New York: MacMillan, 1992, 101-2; Morris, 297.

12 M. McCormick, U. Büntgen, M. A. Cane, E. R. Cook, K. Harper, P. Huybers, T. Litt, S. W. Manning, P. A. Mayewski, A. F. M. More, K. Nicolussi, W. Tegel, "Climate Change during and after the Roman Empire; Reconstructing the past from Scientific and Historical Evidence," *Journal of Interdisciplinary History* XLIII.2 (2012), 169-220. See also M. Rostovtzeff. *Social and Economic History of the Hellenistic World*, vols. I-III. Oxford: Clarendon Press, 1941 (1998 ed.), esp. vol. III, p. 1462 (Chapter V notes), middle of note 20 on precarious grain supplies.

13 R. F. Arragon, "History and the Fall of Rome," *Pacific Historical Review* 1.2 (1932), 145-54.

14 Michael Marshall. "Fall of Roman Empire linked to wild shifts in climate." *New Scientist,* January 13, 2011.

15 Procopius, *History of the Vandal Wars* III.xiv.5-10.

16 Rosen, 2007, 200-03.

17 Gildas, *De Excidio Britonum* 93.3 (*Annnales Cambriae*).

18 M. G. L. Baillie, *A Slice through Time: Dendrochronology and Precision Dating*. London: Batsford, 1995, 95.

19 Ole Benedictow, "The Black Death: The Greatest Catastrophe Ever," *History Today* 55.3 (2005).

20 David Herlihy, *The Black Death and there Transformation of the West*. Cambridge, MA: Harvard University Press, 1997, 96-7.

Bibliography

❖

Abdel-Maksouda, Gomaa and Abdel-Rahman El-Amin. "A Review on the Materials Used During the Mummification Processes in Ancient Egypt." *Mediterranean Archaeology and Archaeometry* 11.2 (2011): 129-50.

Ahituv, Shmuel. "Arad Letters." *Encyclopedia of Hebrew Language and Linguistics,* Leiden: E. J. Brill, 2019.

Akenson, D. H. *Saint Saul: A Skeleton Key to the Historical Jesus.* Oxford: Oxford University Press, 2000.

Albenda, Pauline. *The Palace of Sargon, King of Assyria: Monumental Wall Reliefs at Dur-Sharrukin* (from original drawings made at the time of their discovery in 1843–1844 by Botta and Flandin). Paris: Éditions Recherche sur les civilisations, 1986.

_____. "Dur-Sharrukin, the Royal City of Sargon II, King of Assyria." *Bulletin: Canadian Society for Mesopotamian Studies* 38 (2003): 5-13.

Aldred, Cyril. *Egypt to the End of the Old Kingdom.* New York: McGraw-Hill, 1974.

Apuleius. *The Golden Ass (Metamorphosis).* Jack Lindsay, tr. Bloomington: Indiana University Press, 2005 ed.

Arragon, R. F. "History and the Fall of Rome." *Pacific Historical Review* 1.2 (1932): 145-54.

Asbury, B. "Rethinking Pitt-Rivers." Pitt Rivers Museum, Oxford University, 2013 ((http://web.prm.ox.ac.uk/rpr/index.php/object-biography-index/19-prmcollection/783-flint-knife-188414082/index.html).

Aston, B. G. *Ancient Egyptian stone vessels: materials and forms.* Heidelberger Orientverlag, Heidelberg, 1994.

Bailley, Lloyd R. "The Topography of Hell." *Biblical Archeologist* (1986): 187-91.

Baillie, M. G. L. *A Slice through Time: Dendrochronology and Precision Dating.* London: Batsford, 1995.

Baines, John. "Literacy and Ancient Egyptian Society." *Man: Journal of the Royal Anthropological Institute of Great Britain and Ireland* 18.3 (1983): 572-99.

_____. *Visual and Written Culture in Ancient Egypt.* Oxford: Oxford University Press, 2007, esp. ch. 3, 76-83.

Barkay, G., A.G. Vaughn, M. J. Lundberg and B. Zuckerman, "The Amulets from Ketef Hinnom: A New Edition and Evaluation." *Bulletin of the American Schools of Oriental Research* [*BASOR*] 334 (2004): 41-71.

Barker, Andrew. *Greek Musical Writings I: The Musician and His Art.* Cambridge: Cambridge University Press, 1989 ed.

Barnes, Albert. *Notes on the Old and New Testaments,* vol. 9. *The Gospels,* Baker Books, (originally 1870) 1983.

Barrett, C. K. "Things Sacrificed to Idols." *New Testament Studies* 11.2 (1964-65) 138-53.

Chester Beatty Papyrus. Egyptian Antiquities Department, British Museum, (# EA10683,3).

Benedictow, Ole. "The Black Death: The Greatest Catastrophe Ever." *History Today* 55.3 (2005).

Ben-Tor, Amnon. "Hazor and the Chronology of Northern Israel: A Reply to Israel Finkelstein." *Bulletin of the American Schools of Oriental Research (BASOR)* 317 (2000): 9-15.

Boling, Robert G. *Joshua.* Anchor Yale Bible Commentaries. New Haven: Yale University Press, 1995.

Bookidis, Nancy. "The Sanctuaries of Corinth." *Corinth*, vol. 20. Princeton: American School of Classical Studies, Athens, 2003

Bookidis, Nancy and Ronald Stroud. *Demeter and Persephone in Ancient Corinth.* Princeton: American School of Classical Studies, Athens, 1967.

Bookidis, Nancy, Julie Hansen, Lynn Snyder and Paul Goldberg. "Dining in the Sanctuary of Demeter and Kore at Corinth." *Hesperia: Journal of the American School of Classical Studies at Athens* 66.1 (1999): 1-54.

Borza, Eugene N. "Fire From Heaven: Alexander at Persepolis." *Classical Philology* 67.4 (1972): 233-45.

Bosman, Philip. "The Dodona Bronze Revisited." *Acta Classica* LIX (2016): 184-92.

Bottema, S. "Third Millennium Climate Change in the Near East Based upon Pollen Evidence." *Third Millennium B.C. Climate Change and Old World Collapse,* N. Dalfes, G. Kukla, and H. Weiss, eds, NATO ASI Series 1.49. Berlin: Springer Verlag (1997) 489-515.

Bray, R. S.. *Armies of Pestilence: The Impact of Disease on History.* New York: Barnes and Noble (reprint), 1996.

Brewer, Douglas, Donald Redford and Susan Redford. *Domestic Plants and Animals: The Egyptian Origins.* Warminster: Ars and Phillips, 1994.

Bright, John. *A History of Israel*. Louisville KY: Westminster/John Knox Press, 2000 ed.

Broneer, Oscar. "The Corinthian Isthmus and the Isthmian Sanctuary." *Antiquity* 32.126 (1958): 80-88.

_____. "The Apostle Paul and then Isthmian Games." *Biblical Archeologist* 25.1 (1962): 1-31.

Broshi, M. "The Expansion of Jerusalem in the Reigns of Hezekiah and Manessah." *Israel Exploration Journal* 24.1 (1974) 21-26.

Brown, F., S. R. Driver, C. A. Briggs. *Hebrew and English Lexicon of the Old Testament*. Oxford: Clarendon Press, (1951), 1994 repr.

Bruce, F. F. *The Epistle to the Hebrews*. Grand Rapids: Eerdmans, 1975, 6th pr.

Burckhardt, John Lewis (Johann Ludwig). *Travels in Syria and the Holy Land*. London: Association Promoting the Discovery of the Inner Parts of Africa, 1822 ed. W. M Leake.

Burnett, A. P., "Servants of Peitho: Pindar fr.122 S." *Greek, Roman, Byzantine Studies* 51 (2011): 49-60.

Cahill, Jane. "Jerusalem in David's and Solomon's Time." *Biblical Archaeology Review* 30.6 (2004).

Carlei, Luisa, Simonetta de Felicis Orlandi, Paola Ferraris, Maria Cristina Marhei and Gabriele Borghini, eds. *Marmi Antichi*. Rome: Edizione de Luca, 1997.

Casson, Lionel. *Travel in the Ancient World*. London: Allen and Unwin, 1979.

Clark. Raymond J. "Trophonios: the Manner of His Revelation." *Transactions and Proceedings of the American Philological Association* 99 (1968): 63-75.

Claridge, Amanda. *Rome: Oxford Archaeological Guides.* Oxford University Press, 1998 (2010 printing).

Clifford, Richard. "Phoenician Religion" in *Bulletin of the American Society of Oriental Religion (BASOR)* 279 (1990): 55-64.

Cline, Eric. *From Eden to Exile: Unraveling the Mysteries of the Bible.* Washington, DC: National Geographic, 2007.

_____. *Biblical Archaeology: A Very Short Introduction.* Oxford: Oxford University Press, 2009.

_____. *1177 BC: The Year Civilization Collapsed.* Princeton: Princeton University Press, 2015.

_____. *Three Stones Make a Wall: The Story of Archaeology.* Princeton: Princeton University Press, 2017.

Coarelli, Filippo. *Rome and Environs: An Archaeological Guide.* Berkeley: University of California Press, 2007.

Coldstream, J. N. *Geometric Greece: 900–700 BC.* London: Routledge, 2003, 2nd ed.

Crossan, John Dominic and Jonathan L. Reed. *Excavating Jesus: Beneath the Stones, Behind the Texts.* San Francisco: Harper San Francisco, 2002.

Croy, N. Clayton. "Hellenistic Philosophies and the Preaching of the Resurrection (Acts 17:18, 32)." *Novum Testamentum* 39.1 (1997): 21-39.

Cullen, H. M., P. B. de Menocal, S. Hemming, G. Hemming, F. H. Brown, T. Guilderson, and F. Sirocko. "Climate Change and the Collapse of the Akkadian Empire: Evidence from the Deep Sea." *Journal of Geology* 28 (2000): 79-382.

Cunningham, Andrew and Ole Peter Grell. *Religion, War, Famine and Death in Reformation Europe.* Cambridge: Cambridge University Press, 2001.

Dever William G. Review: "Excavating the Hebrew Bible or Burying It Again?" (Review of *The Bible Unearthed*). *Bulletin of the American Schools of Oriental Research (BASOR)* 322 (2001): 67-77.

De Vries, Keith. "Eighth-Century Corinthian Pottery: Evidence for the Dates of Greek Settlement in the West." *Corinth*, vol. 20. Princeton: American School of Classical Studies, Athens, 2003.

Dieterle, Martina. *Dodona.* Spudasmata Bd. 116. Hildesheim: G. Olms, 2007.

———. "Dodona" in *Blackwell-Wiley Encyclopedia of the Ancient World*, 2012.

Dillon, Matthew. *Omens and Oracles: Divination in Ancient Greece.* London: Routledge, 2017.

Diodorus Siculus. *Bibliotheke Historia* 4. Vol 3, Cambridge, MA: Harvard Loeb, C. H. Oldfather, tr. Vol 3, Harvard Loeb, 4.59-8, 1939.

Disa, J. J., J. Vossoughi, N. H. Goldberg. "A comparison of obsidian and surgical steel scalpel wound healing in rats." *Plastic and Reconstructive Surgery* 92.5 (1993): 884-7.

Doak, B. and C. Lopez-Ruiz, eds. *Oxford Handbook of the Phoenician and Punic Mediterranean.* Oxford: OUP, 2019.

Dothan, Trude and Moshe Dothan. *People of the Sea: The Search for the Philistines.* New York: MacMillan, 1992.

Drews, Robert. *The End of the Bronze Age: Changes in Warfare and the Catastrophe ca. 1200 BC.* Princeton: Princeton University Press, 1993.

Dunbabin, T. J. "The Early History of Corinth." *Journal of Hellenic Studies* 68 (1948): 59-69.

Dunn, James D. G. *Jesus and the Spirit.* SCM Press, 1975.

Editors. "Royal Scribe's 3,000-Year-Old Tomb Discovered in Luxor." *Archaeology* Magazine, February, 2017.

Einhard. *Vita Caroli Magni.* Samuel Turner, tr. Fordham University Sourcebooks.(https://sourcebooks.fordham.edu/basis/einhard.asp), 2019 rev.

Emmett, Chad. "The Capital Cities of Jerusalem." *Geographical Review* 86.2 (1996): 233-58.

Engels, Donald. *Roman Corinth: An Alternative Model for a Classical City.* Chicago: University of Chicago Press, 1990.

Faigenbaum-Golovin, Shira, Arie Shaus, Barak Sober, David Levin, Nadav Na'aman, Benjamin Sass, Eli Turkel, Eli Piasetzky, and Israel Finkelstein. "Algorithmic handwriting analysis of Judah's military correspondence sheds light on composition of biblical texts" *Proceedings of the National Academy of Sciences,* April, 2016.

Fee, Gordon. *First Epistle to the Corinthians* (rev. ed.). Grand Rapids: Eerdmans, 2014.

Feinman, Peter D. *William Foxwell Albright and the Origins of Biblical Archaeology.* Berrien Springs, MI: Andrews University Press, 2004.

Flanagan, James W. "The Relocation of the Davidic Capital." *Journal of the American Academy of Religion* 47.2 1979, 223-44.

Finkel, Irving. *The Ark Before Noah: Decoding the Story of the Flood.* New York: Doubleday/London: Hodder and Stoughton, 2014.

Finkelstein, Israel. *The Archaeology of the Israelite Settlement.* Jerusalem: Israel Exploration Society, 1988.

Finkelstein, Israel and Neil Asher Silberman. *The Bible Unearthed: Archaeology's New Vision of Ancient Israel and the Origin of Sacred Texts.* New York: Simon and Schuster, 2001.

_____. *David and Solomon: In Search of the Bible's Sacred Kings and the Roots of the Western Tradition.* New York: Free Press, 2006.

Finkelstein, Israel. "The Last Labayu: King Saul and the Expansion of the First North Israelite Territorial Entity" in Yairah Amit, Ehud Ben Zvi, Israel Finkelstein, et al., eds. *Essays on Ancient Israel in Its Near Eastern Context: A Tribute to Nadav Na'aman.* Winona Lake: Eisenbrauns, 2006.

_____. *The Quest for the Historical Israel: Archaeology and the History of Early Israel.* Society of Biblical Literature Studies vol. 17. Leiden: E. J. Brill, 2007.

_____. "The 'Large Stone Structure' in Jerusalem: Reality vs. Yearning." *Zeitschrift des Deutschen Palästina Vereins* 127 (2011): 1-11.

Foltz, Richard. "Judaism and the Silk Route." *The History Teacher: Society for History Education* 32.1 (1998): 9-16.

Fontenrose, Joseph. *Python: A Study of Delphic Myth and Its Origins.* Berkeley: University of California Press, 1980.

Forbes, Christopher. "Early Christian Inspired Speech and Hellenistic Popular Religion." *Novum Testamentum* XXXVIII .3 (1986): 257-70.

Fox, Everett et al. *Encyclopedia Judaica* 3, 2007, 2nd ed., 572 ff.

Gadot, Yuval. "Jerusalem and the Holy Land[fill]." *Biblical Archaeology Review*, Jan/Feb 2018.

Galiffa, Federica. "A new faïance alabastron with figurative decoration from Cerveteri." *Abstracts of the Crafts of the European Iron Age Conference*, Cambridge, September 2015.

Galor, Katharina. *Finding Jerusalem: Archaeology Between Science and Ideology.* Berkeley: University of California Press, 2017.

Gardiner, Alan. *The Library of A. Chester Beatty: Description of a Hieratic Papyrus....* London: Oxford University Press, 1931.

_____. *Egyptian Grammar.* Oxford: Griffith Institute, Ashmolean Museum, 1988, Third rev. ed.

Garfinkel, Yosef and Saar Ganor. *Khirbet Qeiyafa Vol. 1. The 2007-2008 Excavation seasons.* Jerusalem: Israel Exploration Society, 2009.

Garnand, Brien. "Phoenicians and Carthaginians in the Western Imagination," in B. Doak and C. Lopez-Ruiz, eds. *Oxford Handbook of the Phoenician and Punic Mediterranean.* Oxford: Oxford University Press, 2019, 697-712.

Garnand, B. K., L. E. Stager and J. A. Greene."Infants as Offerings: Paleodemographic Patterns and Tophet Burial" in P. Xella, ed. *The Tophet in the Phoenician Mediterranean.* Studi Epigrafi Lingistici 30 (2013) 193-222.

Garfinkel, Yosef, Saar Ganor, Michael G. Hasel. *Khirbet Qeiyafa Vol. 2. Excavation Report 2009-2013: Stratigraphy and Architecture (Areas B, C, D, E)*. Jerusalem: Israel Exploration Society, 2014.

Garfinkel, Y. and M. Mumcuoglu. *Solomon's Temple and Palace: New Archaeological Discoveries*. Jerusalem: Korn (Hebrew), 2015.

Germond, Philippe. *An Egyptian Bestiary*. London: Thames and Hudson, 2001.

Graves-Brown, Carolyn. "Flint and Forts: the Role of Flint in Late Middle-New Kingdom Egyptian Weaponry" in T. P. Harrison, E. B Banning and S. Klassen, eds. *Walls of the Prince: Egyptian Interactions with Southwest Asia in Antiquity*, Culture and History of the Ancient Near East Series, Vol. 77, Leiden: E. J. Brill, 2015.

Grayson, A. K. *Assyrian and Babylonian Chronicles*. Locust Valley, NY: J. J. Augustin, 1975 (Winona Lake: Eisenbrauns, 2000).

Grimal, Nicholas. *A History of Ancient Egypt*, tr. Ian Shaw. Oxford: Blackwell, 1972.

Hafford, W. B. "Mesopotamian Mensuration Balance Pan Weights from Nippur." *Journal of the Economic and Social History of the Orient* 48.3 (2005): 345-87.

Hammond, N. G. L. *Sources for Alexander the Great*. Cambridge: Cambridge University Press, 1993.

Harding, G. Lankester. "The Story of Frankincense." *Saudi Aramco World*, Jan/Feb, 1965, 24-27.

Harris, W. "Sounding Brass and Hellenistic Technology." *Biblical Archaeology Review* 8.1 (1982)

Herlihy, David. *The Black Death and the Transformation of the West.* Cambridge, MA: Harvard University Press, 1997.

Herodotus *History* 2. A. D. Godley, tr. *The Persian Wars.* Books I-II. Cambridge MA: Harvard Loeb 1999 ed.

Holmes, Seth. "Dyeing Bronze: New Evidence for an Old Reading of *Agamemnon* 612," *Classical Quarterly* 62.2 (2012): 486-95.

Hom, M. K. Y. H. "Where Art Thou, O Hezekiah's Tunnel… [Waterworks]" *Journal of Biblical Literature* 135.3 (2016): 493-503.

Hunt, Patrick N. "Bronze Tabulae Ansatae at Roman Summus Poeninus in the Roman Alps." *Acta II, From the Parts to the Whole: XIIIth International Bronze Congress Proceedings 1996*, vol. 2. Harvard University Art Museums, *Journal of Roman Archaeology Supplement*, 2002.

_____. "Egyptian Kingship amd Animal Husbandry." *Electrum Magazine.* June 2014. (http://www.electrummagazine.com/2014/06/egyptian-kingship-and-animal-husbandry/).

_____. "Four Horsemen of the Apocalypse: from Paleoclimates to the Present." *Philolog* (Stanford) Jan., 2009 (http://traumwerk.stanford.edu/philolog/2009/02/four_horsemen_of_the_apocalyps.html *original* html but not all these html have transferred to the permanent Stanford servers.).

_____. *Hannibal.* New York: Simon & Schuster, 2017.

_____. "Imperium and Genius in the Pantheon of Rome." Electrum Magazine. May, 2016. (http://www.electrummagazine.com/2016/05/imperium-and-genius-in-the-pantheon-of-rome/).

_____. "Irony and Realism in the Iconography of Caravaggio's Penitent Magdalene", chapter 6, in M. A. Erhardt and A. M. Morris, eds., *Mary Magdalene, Iconographic Studies from the Middle Ages to the Baroque.* Studies in Religion and the Arts, vol. 7. Leiden: E. J. Brill, 2012, 161-86.

_____. "Mt. Saphon in Myth and Fact" in E. Lipinski, ed. *Phoenicia and the Bible.* Studia Phoenicia XI. *Orientalia Lovanensia Analecta* 44, Leuven: Uitgeverij Peeters, 1991, 103-15.

_____. "Pantheon" in *Encyclopedia of the Ancient World.* Salem Press, 2002, 868.

_____. "Plant Technology and Science in Antiquity." *Blackwell's A Cultural History of Plants,* vol. 1: Antiquity. Annette Giesecke, ed. London: Blackwell-Wiley, forthcoming 2021.

_____. *Provenance, Weathering and Technology of Selected Archaeological Basalts and Andesites.* Ph.D. Dissertation, Institute of Archaeology, UCL (U. London): 1991.

_____. "Roman Mansio, Plan de Barasson" *Vallesia* LIV *:* Recherches Archeologiques dans le Canton du Valais, ed. Francois Wible (1999): 300-8.

_____. "Sensory Images in Song of Songs 1:2-2:16" in M. Augustin and K.-D. Schunck, eds. *"Dort ziehen Schiffe dahin..." Beiträge zur Erforschung des Alten Testaments und des Antiken Judentums* 28. Frankfurt am Main: Peter Lang Verlag, 1996, 69-78, esp. 70-1.

_____. "Subtle Paronomasia in the *Canticum Canticorum*: Hidden Treasures of the Superlative Poet" in K.-D. Schunck and M. Augustin, eds. *Goldene Äpfel in silbernen Schalen. Beiträge zur Erforschung des Alten Testaments und des Antiken Judentums* 20. Frankfurt am Main: Peter Lang Verlag, 1992, 147-54.

_____. "Summus Poeninus on the Great Bernard Pass." *Journal of Roman Archaeology* XI (1998): 264-71.

_____. *Ten Discoveries That Rewrote History*. New York: Plume/Penguin Group, 2007.

_____. "Triptolemos and Beyond in the Stanford Kleophon Krater." *Stanford Museum Journal*, Cantor Arts Center, 2001, 3-8.

Hunt, Patrick and Andreaa Seicean. "Alpine Archaeology and Paleopathology: Was Hannibal's Army also decimated by epidemic while crossing the Alps?" *Archaeolog* (Stanford) May 20, 2007. https://web.stanford.edu/dept/archaeology/cgi-bin/archaeolog/?p=123.

Jackson, Ralph. *Doctors and Diseases in the Roman Empire*. London: British Museum Press, 1991.

Jacobson, D. M. and M. P. Weitzmann. "What Was Corinthian Bronze?" *American Journal of Archaeology* 96.2 (1992): 237-47.

Jacobson, David M. "Corinthian Bronze and the Gold of the Alchemists." *Gold Bulletin* 33.2 (2000): 60-66.

Jashemski, Wilhelmina and F. G. Meyer, eds. *The Natural History of Pompeii*. Cambridge: Cambridge University Press, 2002.

Joffe, A. H. "The Rise of Secondary States in the Iron Age Levant." *Journal of the Economic and Social History of the Orient* 45.4 (2002): 425-67.

Jones, Peter. "Experimental Butchery with Modern Stone Tools and Its Relevance for Palaeolithic Archaeology." *World Archaeology* 12.2 (1988): 153-65.

Jordan, William C. *The Great Famine: Northern Europe in the Early Fourteenth Century.* Princeton: Princeton University Press, 1996.

Josephus, *Wars of the Jews.* William Whiston, ed., Samuel Burder, rev. *The Genuine Works of Flavius Josephus.* London: Albion Press, 1812.

_____. *The Jewish War.* New York: Penguin Classics, 1984 reissue.

Katz, Nathan. "From Legend to History: India and Israel in the Ancient World." *Shofar: Interdisciplinary Journal of Jewish Studies* 17.3 (Special Issue: Judaism and Asian Religions) (1999): 7-22.

Kent, John Harvey. *Corinth VIII, Part III, The Inscriptions 1926-50.* Princeton: American School of Classical Studies, Athens, 1966.

Kenyon, Kathleen. "Ancient Jerusalem." *Scientific American* 213.1 (1965): 84-91.

Kerenyi, C. *Eleusis: Archetypal Image of Mother and Daughter.* Princeton: Princeton University Press, 1967.

King, Philip J. "Travel, Transport, Trade." *Eretz-Israel* 26 (1999) Israel Exploration Society, 94-105.

Kitchen, Kenneth. "Where Did King Solomon's Gold Go?" *Biblical Archaeology Review* 15.3 (1989): 30.

_____. *The Third Intermediate Period in Egypt: 1100-650 BC.* (Aris and Phillips Classical Texts). Liverpool: University of Liverpool Press, 1996.

_____. *On the Reliability of the Old Testament.* Grand Rapids MI: Eerdmans, 2006.

Klein, Konstantin. "Wo Josephine sich einst verkohlte" (Karlsthron). *Archäologische Kolloquium*, Universität Bamberg May 15, 2007.

Klein, W. W. "Noisy Gong or Acoustic Vase?" *New Testament Studies* 32 (1986): 286-9.

Knapp, A. Bernard and Sturt Manning. "Crisis in Context: the End of the Late Bronze Age in the Eastern Mediterranean." *American Journal of Archaeology* 120.1 (2016): 99-149.

Knott, Elizabeth. "The Middle Babylonian / Kassite Period (ca. 1595–1155 B.C.) in Mesopotamia." *Heilbrunn Timeline of Art History*. New York: The Metropolitan Museum of Art, 2000–. http://www.metmuseum.org/toah/hd/kass/hd_kass.htm (June 2016); "Assyria, 1365–609 B.C." Department of Ancient Near Eastern Art. In *Heilbrunn Timeline of Art History*. New York: The Metropolitan Museum of Art, 2000–. http://www.metmuseum.org/toah/hd/assy/hd_assy.htm (originally published October 2004).

Koester, Craig R. *Revelation: A New Translation and Commentary*. Anchor Yale Bible Commentaries. New Haven: Yale University Press, 2015.

Kohler, Kaufmann and Ludwig Blau. "Gehenna" in the *Jewish Encyclopedia* (1906 edition).

La Niece, Susan and Paul Craddock. *Metal Plating and Patination: Cultural, Technical and Historical developments*. Blackwell/Elsevier, 2017.

Layard, Austen Henry. *Nineveh and its Remains…*London: John Murray, 1849.

_____. Austen Henry Layard. *The Monuments of Nineveh: From Drawings Made on the Spot, First Series*. London: John Murray, 1849.

Lelièvre, Francine, James Snyder, Joel King, eds. *Archaeology from King David to the Dead Sea Scrolls. Collaborative Exhibition in the Montréal Museum of Archaeology and History and the Israel Museum.* Jerusalem, 2003.

Lepie, Herta and Georg Minkenberg. *The Cathedral Treasury of Aachen.* Schnell–Steiner, Regensburg, 2013, 2nd ed.

Levy, Thomas et al. "High-precision radiocarbon dating and historical biblical archaeology in southern Jordan." *Proceedings of the National Academy of Science* 105 [43] October 28, 2008, 16460-16465.

Lichtheim, Miriam. *Egyptian Literature,* vol. II. New Kingdom. Berkeley: University of California Press, 1976.

Liddell, H. G. and R. Scott. *A Greek-English Lexicon.* Oxford: Clarendon Press, 1996 rev.

Lightfoot, Christopher et al. *Ennion: Master of Roman Glass.* Metropolitan Museum of Art, New York, 2015.

Lipp, E. K., A. Huq, R. R. Colwell. "Effects of global climate on in factious disease: the cholera model." *Clinical Microbiology Reviews* 15.4 (2002): 757-70.

Liverani, M., "The collapse of the Near Eastern regional system at the end of the Bronze Age: the case of Syria," in *Centre and Periphery in the Ancient World,* M. Rowlands, M.T. Larsen, K. Kristiansen, eds. Cambridge: Cambridge University Press, 1987.

Lo Cascio, Elio. "The Size of the Roman Population: Beloch and the Meaning of the Augustan Census Figures." *Journal of Roman Studies* 84 (1994): 23-40.

Luckenbill, D. D. *Ancient Records of Assyria and Babylon*, vol. 2. Oriental Institute Chicago: University of Chicago Press, 1927.

MacNeill, William H. "Infectious Alternatives: the Plague that Saved Jerusalem" in Robert Cowley, ed. *What If?—The World's Foremost Military Historians Imagine What Might Have Been*. New York: G. P. Putnam's Sons, 1999, 1-14.

Malamat, Abraham. *History of Biblical Israel: Major Problems and Minor Issues*. Leiden: E. J. Brill, 2001.

Magness, Jodi. *The Archaeology of Qumran and the Dead Sea Scrolls (Studies in the Dead Sea Scrolls and Related Literature)*. Grand Rapids MI: Eerdmans, 2002.

_____. *The Archaeology of the Holy Land: From the Destruction of Solomon's Temple to the Muslim Conquest*. Cambridge: Cambridge University Press, 2012.

Marcus, Joel. *Mark 8-16*. Anchor Yale Bible Commentaries. New Haven: Yale University Press, 2009.

Marshall, Michael. "Fall of Roman Empire linked to wild shifts in climate." *New Scientist,* January 13, 2011.

Martin, I. J. "Glossalalia in the Apostolic Church." *Journal of Biblical Literature* 63.2 (1944): 123-30.

Masson, A. "Le quartier des prêtres du temple de Karnak: rapport préliminaire de la fouille de la maison VII, 2001-2003." *Cahiers de Karnak* XII, 2007, 593-655, esp. 612, plate XXVIII no. 1-3.

Master, Daniel. "Economy and Exchange in the Iron Age Kingdoms of the Southern Levant." *Bulletin of the American Schools of Oriental Research* (*BASOR*) 372 (2014): 81-97.

Mattusch, Carol C. *Greek Bronze Statuary: From the Beginnings Through the Fifth Century BC.* Ithaca: Cornell University Press, 1988.

_____. *Classical Bronzes: Art and Craft of Greek and Roman Statuary.* Ithaca: Cornell University Press, 1996.

_____. "Corinthian Bronze—famous but elusive." *Corinth,* vol. 20. Princeton: American School of Classical Studies, Athens, 2003.

May, L. Carlyle. "A Survey of Glossalalia and Related Phenomena in Non-Christian Religions." *American Anthropologist* (NS) 58.1 (1956): 75-96.

Mazar, Amihai. *Archaeology in the Land of the Bible.* New York: Anchor Doubleday, 1992.

_____. *Excavations at Tell Qasile, Part Two. Various Finds, The Pottery, Conclusions, Appendices* (*Qedem* 20). Jerusalem: The Hebrew University of Jerusalem, 1985

_____. "Does Amihai Mazar Agree with Finkelstein's Low Chronology?" *Biblical Archaeology Review* 29.2 (2003).

Mazar, Eilat. "Did I Find King David's Palace?" *Biblical Archaeology Review* 32.1 (2006).

McCarty, M. M. "Africa Punica? Child Sacrifice and Other Invented Traditions in Early Roman Africa." *Religion in the Roman Empire* 3.3 (2017) 393-428.

McCormick, M., U. Büntgen, M. A. Cane, E. R. Cook, K. Harper, P. Huybers, T. Litt, S. W. Manning, P. A. Mayewski, A. F. M. More, K. Nicolussi, W. Tegel. "Climate Change during and after the Roman Empire; Reconstructing the past from Scientific and Historical Evidence." *Journal of Interdisciplinary History* XLIII.2 (2012): 169-220.

McGovern, Patrick. *Ancient Brews: Rediscovered and Recreated.* New York: W. W. Norton and Company, 2017.

Meeks, Wayne. *The First Urban Christians.* New Haven: Yale University Press, 1983.

Merker, Gloria. *The Sanctuary of Demeter and Kore: Terracotta Figurines of the Classical, Hellenistic and Roman Periods. Corinth,* vol. 18. Princeton: American School of Classical Studies, Athens, 2000.

Meyer, Eric M. "Early Judaism and Christianity in the Light of Archaeology." *Biblical Archaeologist* 51.2 (1988): 69-79.

_____, ed. *The Oxford Encyclopedia of Archaeology in the Near East.* vols. 1-5. Oxford: Oxford University Press, 1996.

_____. "The Torah Shrine in the Ancient Synagogue: Another Look at the Evidence." *Jewish Studies Quarterly* 4.4 (1997): 303-38.
Middleton, Guy D. "Nothing Lasts Forever: Environmental Discourses on the collapse of Past Societies." *Journal of Archaeological Research* 20 (2012): 257-307.

Millard, Alan R. "Does the Bible Exaggerate King Solomon's Golden Wealth?" *Biblical Archaeology Review* 15.3 (1989): 20-29.

_____. *Reading and Writing in the Time of Jesus.* New York: New York University Press, 2000.

Mitchell, T. C. *The Bible in the British Museum: Interpreting the Evidence.* London: British Museum Press, 2004.

Monson, James. *The Land Between: A Regional Study Guide to the Land of the Bible.* Jerusalem: Biblical Backgrounds, 1996.

Morley, Neville. *Metropolis and hinterland: the city of Rome and the Italian economy 200 B.C.–A.D. 200.* Cambridge: Cambridge University Press, 1996.

Morris, Ian. *Why The West Rules—For Now.* New York: Farrar, Straus, Giroux, 2010.

Morris, J. Glenn. "Cholera: Modern Pandemic Disease of Ancient Lineage." *Emerging Infectious Diseases* vol. 17 (11) November, 2011, 2099-2104.

Muller, Kristina. "Mummies and Surgery: The Story of Ancient Egyptian Obsidian Scalpels." *MedicalExpo* June 9, 2015 (http://emag. medicalexpo.com/article-long/mummies-and-surgery-the-story-of-ancient-egyptian-obsidian-scalpels/).

Myers, Jacob M. *II Chronicles.* Anchor Yale Bible Commentaries. New Haven: Yale University Press, 1995.

Mylonas, George. *Eleusis and the Eleusinian Mysteries.* Princeton: Princeton University Press, 1961.

Nasrallah, L. S. *Archaeology and the Letters of Paul.* Oxford: Oxford University Press, 2019.

Nam, Roger. *Portrayals of Economic Exchange in the Book of Kings.* Leiden: E. J. Brill, 2012.

Nelson, E. J., J. B. Harris, J. Glenn Morris, S. B. Calderwood, A. Camilli. "Cholera Transmission: the Host, pathogen and bacteriophage dynamic." *Nature Reviews Microbiology* 7 (2009): 693-702.

Newton, Derek. "Food Offered to Idols in I Corinthians 8-10: A Study of Conflicting Viewpoints in the Setting of Religious Pluralism in Corinth." Ph.D. Dissertation, Sheffield, 1995.

Noegel, Scott. "On Puns and Divination: Egyptian Dream Exegesis from a Comparative Perspective" in Kasia Spkakowska, ed., *Through a Glass Darkly: Magic, Dreams and Prophecy in Ancient Egypt.* Classical Press of Wales, 2006, ch. 6, 95-120.

Noy, Tamar, Joseph Schuldenrein, and Eitan Tchernov. "Gilgal, A Pre-Pottery Neolithic Site in the Lower Jordan Valley." *Israel Exploration Journal* 30.1/2 (1980): 63-82.

_____. "Gilgal I—A Pre-Pottery Neolithic Site, Israel,—the 1985-97 Seasons." *Paléorient* 15.1 (1989) Colloque Préhistoire Levant II, 1988, Editions de CNRS, Paris, 1989, 11-18.

O'Connor, Jerome Murphy. "Corinthian Bronze." *Revue Biblique* 90 (1983) 80-91.

_____. *I Corinthians.* Anchor Bible Commentary. New York: Anchor / Doubleday, 1998.

Orlinsky, Harry. "The Plain Meaning of RUACH in Gen. 1:2," *Jewish Quarterly Review* 48.2 (1957): 174-82.

Orr, William F. *I Corinthians.* Anchor Yale Bible Commentaries. New Haven: Yale University Press, 1995.

Parke, H. W. *The Oracles of Zeus.* Oxford: Blackwell, 1967.

Parkinson, R. B. "Sinuhe's Dreaming[s]: The Text and Meanings of a Simile" in Kasia Spkakowska, ed., *Through a Glass Darkly: Magic, Dreams and Prophecy in Ancient Egypt.* Classical Press of Wales, 2006, ch. 8, 145-74.

Pausanias. *Description of Greece, Book 2.* Vol. 1 Books 1-2. W. H. S. Jones, tr. Cambridge MA: Harvard Loeb, 1918 rev.

Pedley, J. G. *New Light on Ancient Carthage*, University of Michigan Press, 1990.

Peterson, L. H. *The Places of Roman Isis: Between Egyptomania, Politics and Religion.* Oxford Handbooks. Oxford: Oxford University Press, 2016.

Petrie, W. M. Flinders. *Tools and Weapons Illustrated by the Egyptian Collection, University College, London.* British School of Archaeology in Egypt, 1916.

Pharr, Clyde. *Vergil's Aeneid Books I-VI.* Lexington, MA: D. C. Heath, rev. ed. 1964,

Pillinger, Emily. *Cassandra and the Poetics of Prophecy in Greek and Latin Literature.* Cambridge: Cambridge University Press, 2019.

Pioske, Daniel. "David's Jerusalem" A Sense of Place." *Near Eastern Archaeology* 76.1 (2013): 4-15.

Plato. *Apologia* 32. H. N. Fowler, tr. Cambridge: MA: Harvard Loeb, 1990 ed.

Pliny. *Natural History*, vol. IV Books 12-16, vol. IX. Books 33-35. H. Rackham, tr. Cambridge MA: Harvard Loeb, 1945, 1952.

Iulii Pollucis. *Onomasticon*, vol. I (ed. W. Dindorf) Leipzig: Libraria Kuehniana, 1824, 103-4, 436.

Prada, Luigi. "Dreams, Bilingualism, and Oneiromancy in Ptolemaic Egypt: remarks on a recent Study." *Zeitschrift für Papyrologie und Epigraphik* Bd. 184 (2013): 85-101.

Pritchard, J. B. *Ancient Near Eastern Texts.* Princeton: Princeton University Press, 1969, 3rd ed.

Procopius: The Secret History with Related Texts. Anthony Kaldellis, ed./ tr. Indianapolis: Hackett, 2010.

Provan, Iain, ed. *New Annotated Oxford Bible* (II *Kings* 19:35-6). Oxford: Oxford University Press, 3rd ed., 1991, 566.

Quirk, Stephen and Jeffrey Spencer, eds. *The British Museum Book of Ancient Egypt.* London: Thames and Hudson / British Museum Press, 2001 ed.

Race, W. H. *Pindar: Nemean Odes, Isthmian Odes, Fragments.* Loeb Classics, Cambridge: Harvard University Press, 1997.

Ray, John. *The Archive of Hor.* (Excavations at North Saqqara) Ostraka Texts. London: Egyptian Exploration Society, 1976, 130-6.

Rendsburg, Gary. "Word Play in Biblical Hebrew" in Scott Noegel, ed. *Puns and Pundits: Word Play in the Hebrew Bible and Ancient Near Eastern Literature.* Bethesda, MD: CDL Press, 2000.

Rendsburg, G. A. and W. M. Schniedewind. "The Siloam Tunnel Inscription: Historical and Linguistic Perspectives." *Israel Exploration Journal* 60 (2010): 188-203.

_____. *How the Bible is Written.* Peabody, MA: Hendrickson Publishing, 2019.

Roberts, C. A. "Palaeopathology and its relevance to understanding health and disease today: the impact of the environment on health, past and present." *Anthropological Review* (De Gruyter) 79.1 (2016): 1-16.

Rosen, William. *Justinian's Flea: The First Great Plague and the End of the Roman Empire.* London: Viking/Penguin, 2007.

_____. *The Third Horseman: Climate Change and the Great Famine of the 14th Century.* London: Viking/Penguin, 2014.

Rosner, Brian S. "Temple Prostitution in I Corinthians 6:12-20." *Novum Testamentum* 40.4 (1998) 336-51.

Rostker, Bernard. *Providing for the Casualties of War.* Santa Monica CA: Rand Corporation, 2013.

Rostovtzeff, M. *Social and Economic History of the Hellenistic World,* 3. Vol. Oxford: Clarendon Press, 1941, (1998 ed.).

Rundle, Clark R. T. *Myth and Symbol in Ancient Egypt.* London: Thames and Hudson, 1991.

Sagrillo, T. L. "Šišak's army: 2 Chronicle 12:2-3" in *Culture and History, Proceedings of the Int'l. Conference, University of Haifa May 2-5 2010.* Münster: Ugarit-Verlag, 425-50.

Schachter, Albert. "A Boeotian Cult Type." *Bulletin of the Institute of Classical Studies* 14 (1967): 1-16.

Shaw, Ian and Paul Nicholson, eds. *The Dictionary of Ancient Egypt.* London: Abrams and British Museum Press, 1995.

Scheidel, Walter. "Roman population size: the logic of the debate." *Princeton—Stanford Working Papers in Classics 2.0.* Princeton, NJ, 2007.

Schütte, Sven. "Der Aachener Thron" in M. Kramp (Ed.): *Krönungen, Könige in Aachen—Geschichte und Mythos.* Verlag Philipp von Zabern, 1999.

Schwartz, Jeffrey, Frank Houghton, Roberto Machiarelli and Luca Bondioli. "Skeletal Remains from Punic Carthage Do Not Support Systematic Sacrifice of Infants." *PLoS (Public Library of Science)* 5, # 2, (February 17, 2010) e9177.

Scobie, Alex. "Rich and Poor in the Roman World, 50 BC–AD 150" *Classical Outlook 60.2* (1982) 44-46.

Scott, David A.. "The Deterioration of Gold Alloys and Some Aspects of Their Conservation." *Studies in Conservation 28.4* (1983) 194-203.

Sherratt, Susan and Andrew. "The Growth of the Mediterranean Economy in the Early First Millennium BC." *World Archaeology* 24.3 (1993): 361-78.

Shimron, A.E. and A. Frumkin, "The Why How and When of the Siloam Tunnel Ree valuated: A Reply." *Bulletin of the American Schools of Oriental Research* 364 (2011): 53-60.

Siani-Davies, M. "Ptolemy XII Auletes and the Romans." *Historia: Zeitschrift fur Alte Geschichte* Bd. 46. H. 3,3 (1997): 306-40.

Smith, Adam T. "The Making of an Urartian Landscape in Southern Transcaucasia: A Study of Political Architectonics." *American Journal of Archaeology* 103.1 (1999): 45-71.

Smith, Amy and Sadie Pickup, eds. *Brill's Companion to Aphrodite.* Leiden: E. J. Brill, 2010.

Smith, D. E. "The Egyptian Cults at Corinth." *Harvard Theological Review* 70.3/4 (1977): 201-31.

Soren, David, Aicha Ben Abed Ben Khader, Hedi Slim. *Carthage; Uncovering the Mysteries and Splendors of Ancient Tunisia.* New York: Simon and Schuster, 1990.

Speiser, E. A. *Genesis.* Anchor Yale Bible Commentaries. New Haven: Yale University Press, 2nd ed., 1963.

Sperveslage, Gunnar. "Intercultural Contacts between Egypt and the Arabian Peninsula at the turn off the 2nd to 1st millennium BCE" in *Dynamics of Production in the Ancient Near East: 1300–500 BC.* J. C. Moreno Garcia, ed. Oxford: Oxbow Books, 2016, ch. 14.

Stager, L. E. "A View from the Tophet" in *Phönizer im Westen*, Philip von Zabern, 1982, 155-66.

Stager, L. and S. Wolff. "Child sacrifice at Carthage: Religious Rite for Population Control?" *Biblical Archaeology Review* 10 (1984): 30-51.

Stager, Lawrence E. "The Rite of Child Sacrifice at Carthage," in J. G. Pedley, *New Light on Ancient Carthage*, University of Michigan Press, 1990, 1-11.

Stead, Miriam. *Egyptian Life.* London: British Museum Press, 1994.

Stewart, Stanley. "In Search of the Real Queen of Sheba." *National Geographic News,* Dec. 3, 2018 (https://www.nationalgeographic.com/travel/destinations/africa/ethiopia/mysterious-queen-sheba-legend-church-archaeology/).

Strabo. *Geography.* H. L. Jones, tr. Vol IV, Cambridge MA: Harvard University Press, 1927.

Swaddling, Judith. *Olympic Games.* London: British Museum Press, 2001 repr.

Thistleton, Anthony C. *The First Epistle to the Corinthians.* Grand Rapids: Eerdmans, 2013.

Svarlien, Diane Arnson. Pindar *Isthmean.* (1990), also *The Odes of Pindar*, in Perseus Project 1.0, Yale University Press, 1991.

Torrence, R., C. Pavlides, P. Jackson and J. Webb. "Volcanic Disasters and Cultural Discontinuities in Holocene Time in West New Britain, Papua New Guinea" in W. J. McGuire, D. R. Griffiths, P. L. Hancock and I. S. Stewart, eds. *The Archaeology of Geological Catastrophes.* Geological Society Special Publication no. 171. London: Geological Society of London, 2000, 225-44.

Trentinella, Rosemary. "Roman Glass." Metropolitan Museum of Art, *Heilbrunn Timeline of Art History,* 2003.

Trigger, Bruce. *A History of Archaeological Thought.* 2nd ed. Cambridge: Cambridge University Press, 2006.

Tsumura, D. F. *The Earth and The Waters in Genesis 1 and 2: A Linguistic Investigation.* Sheffield: JSOT Press, 1989.

Tubb, Jonathan and Rupert Chapman. *Archaeology and the Bible.* London: British Museum Press, 1990.

Tubb, Jonathan. "Editorial: Early Iron Age Judah in the Light of Recent Discoveries at Khirbet Qeiyafa." *Palestine Exploration Quarterly* 142 (2009): 1-2.

Van Beek, Gus. "Frankincense and Myrrh." *Biblical Archaeologist* 23.3 (1960): 69-95.

van der Mieroop, Marc. *A History of the Ancient Near East ca. 3000–323 BC.* Oxford: Blackwell, 2006.

Villing, Alexandra, Marianne Bergeron, Giorgos Bourogiannis, Alan Johnston, François Leclère, Aurélia Masson and Ross Thomas. *Naukratis: Greeks in Egypt,* "The Material Culture at Naukratis: An Overview." British Museum (https://research.britishmuseum.org/pdf/ Naukratis_ORC_Material_Culture_Villing_Bergeron_Johnston_ Masson_Thomas.pdf).

Voltaire, *Philosophy of History,* X, Of the Chaldees, 1765.

Wallis Budge, E. A.. *The Gods of the Egyptians,* vol. 1. Studies in Egyptian Mythology. London: Methuen, 1904, Chapter XIV, "Hathor and the Hathor Goddesses."

Wallis Budge, E. A. T., edited by John Romer. *The Egyptian Book of the Dead.* London: Penguin Books, 2008 ed.

Walsh, J. J. *The Great Fire of Rome: Life and Death in the Ancient City.* Baltimore: Johns Hopkins University Press, 2019.

Weinberg, Saul S. "The Geometric and Orientalizing Pottery." *Corinth,* vol. 7.1. Princeton: American School of Classical Studies, Athens (1943), pp. i-xiv.

Weiss, Barry. "The Decline of Late Bronze Age Civilization as a Possible Response to Climatic Change." *Climate Change* 4.2 (1982): 173-98.

Westall, Richard. "The Loan to Ptolemy XII, 59-48 BCE". *Ricerche di Egittologia e di Antichità* Copte (*REAC* 12) (2010).

Williams, R. J. "Scribal Training in Ancient Egypt." *Journal of the American Oriental Society* 92.2 (1972): 214-21.

Wilson, A. N. *Paul: The Mind of the Apostle.* New York: W. W. Norton and Co., 1997.

Wiseman, Donald and Edwin Yamauchi. *Archaeology and the Bible: An Introductory Study.* Grand Rapids: Eerdmans, 1979.

Witherington, Ben. *Conflict and Community in Corinth: A Socio-Rhetorical Commentary on 1 and 2 Corinthians.* Grand Rapids: Eerdmans, 1995

Wright, N. T. *Paul: A Biography*. New York: Harper, 2018.

Xella, Paolo, ed. *The Tophet in the Phoenician Mediterranean*. Studi Epigrafi e Linguistici 30 (2013)

Xella, Paolo, Quinn, Josephine, Melchiorri, Valentina and Van Dommelen, Peter. "Phoenician Bomes of Contention." *Antiquity* 87 (2013) 1199-1207

Yamauchi, Edwin. *The Stones and the Scriptures*. Philadelphia: J. B. Lippincott and Company, 1972.

Zimansky, Paul. "Xenophon and the Urartian Legacy." *Pallas* 43 (1995): 255-68.

About the Author

❖

Patrick Hunt is an archaeologist and historian. His Ph.D. is in Archaeology from the Institute of Archaeology, UCL, (University of London), 1991. He has been teaching at Stanford University since 1993 after being a Visiting Scholar in Classics there in 1992. He was a post-doctoral Research Fellow in Near Eastern Studies at the University of California, Berkeley (1992-94) under Professor David Stronach. Some of his field research has been sponsored by National Geographic Expedition Council (2007-08) as a grantee and he is an Expeditions Expert for National Geographic Expeditions (since 2016). He is also an elected Fellow of the Royal Geographical Society (1989) and an elected Fellow of the Explorers Club in New York.

Hunt has authored 22 published books, including *Hannibal* (Simon and Schuster, 2017) and *Ten Discoveries That Rewrote History* (Penguin Group, 2007). He has also authored over 100 peer-reviewed articles (including in biblical studies) for *Phoenicia and the Bible – Studia Phoenicia* XI (1991), the *Journal of Roman Archaeology XI* (1998*)*, *Encyclopaedia Britannica* (10 articles since 2016), *Beiträge zur Erforschung des Alten Testaments und des Antiken Judentums* Bands 20 & 28 (Peter Lang Verlag, Frankfurt 1992, 1996), *World Archaeology* 21.1 (1989) as well as for E. J. Brill in Leiden (2012), the *Blackwell-Wiley Encyclopedia of the Ancient World*, (2012), and *Blackwell's Cultural History of Plants* (Antiquity, vol. 1) forthcoming in 2021. In 1993 he was named to and listed in *Who's Who in Biblical Studies and Archaeology* by the Biblical Archaeology Society.

Hunt has taught "Archaeology and the Bible" as a course many times in the last three decades. He has lived in Israel, Greece, Italy and the UK (London) and also conducted annual fieldwork in Europe as well as in the Near East since 1984. Hunt is also a National Lecturer for the Archaeological Institute of America (AIA) since 2009, President of the Stanford AIA Society (current), and past President of the California Classical Association NS (1986). Hunt is a frequent featured scholar for PBS, National Geographic and NOVA documentaries.